A PRIMER FOR TEACHING
WORLD HISTORY

—— Ten Design Principles ——

Antoinette Burton

DUKE UNIVERSITY PRESS
Durham & London
2012

© 2012 Duke University Press
All rights reserved
Printed in the United States of America on
acid-free paper ∞
Designed by Jennifer Hill
Typeset in Garamond Premier Pro by
Tseng Information Systems, Inc.

Library of Congress
Cataloging-in-Publication Data
appear on the last printed page of
this book.

For Nick and Olivia
World travelers, midwestern kids

——— *Contents* ———

———— Acknowledgments ————

THOUGH I STARTED my life as a practicing historian by prepping lectures for a Western Civilization course in a summer night-school program, I have been shaped immeasurably in both my teaching and my research careers by my first world history assignment at Indiana State University. It was 1990, and one year into my stint there the First Gulf War started — a global geography lesson and so much more. I taught two sections of "world civilizations" each semester for three years, and in that context my formative training in the project of global history took place. Teaching those courses made a huge impression on me, and it's not too much to say that I come back to that experience every time I sit down to revise my world history syllabus or write a new lecture. Since then, students and colleagues at the University of Illinois have shaped my apprehensions of world history, and I feel deeply indebted to those students and colleagues as well. With Peter Fritzsche and Tony Ballantyne, I coorganized an NEH seminar on globalization and teaching world history, whence many of the principles and commitments in evidence here germinated. Ann Klotz and teachers at the Laurel School heard very early versions of some of the ideas here; I am grateful to Ann and her faculty for their experience and feedback, as I am to Steve Buenning of William Fremd High School in Palatine, Illinois, who read parts of the primer in draft and offered sage advice.

I've had conversations about teaching too numerous to count with Jean Allman, Clare Crowston, Augusto Espiritu, Behrooz Ghamari, Kathy Oberdeck, Dana Rabin, Anna Bateman, Amanda Brian, Nathan Chio, Debbie Hughes, Danielle Kinsey, Becky Nickerson, Zack Poppel, Karen Rodriguez'G, Emily Skidmore, Carol Symes, and Jamie Warren. Clare Crowston, Stephanie Foote, Fred Hoxie, Lynn Hunt, Laura Mayhall, Dana Rabin, Mrinalini Sinha, Heather Streets-Salter, and two very astute readers for Duke University Press all gave me invaluable feedback on the manuscript; I am so grateful to them. Marilyn Lake reminded me of my own geopolitical position and shared many fruitful insights as well. John Randolph also read parts of the manuscript; he and Dianne Harris and Ray Fouché have kept me honest about digital humanities and honed my thinking about its possibilities for world history teaching. My conversations with Siobhan Somerville about all kinds of questions — gender, sexuality, politics, and struggle — have also left their imprint here, as has her friendship. Vicki Burton is as passionate a teacher as I know, and we have struggled together with worldly issues in ways that have left me sharper and wiser, for which I am truly grateful. T. J. Tallie has read and engaged with every single word, chai included, for which I thank him. Thanks as well to Fred Hoxie and Kristin Hoganson for modeling the Hot Seat exercise for me and to Marie Ciavarella of the College of Liberal Arts and Sciences Teaching Academy for letting us talk out loud about it. Tony Ballantyne is as good an interlocutor and as informed a practitioner of world history as one could ever hope for; thanks to him for years of collegiality and friendship.

Miriam Angress is simply, continually, amazing. A writer with a creative life of her own, she never fails to witness the world in the pebbles I lay before her, and to rejoice in them with me as a friend as well as an editor. Paul is the ultimate IT go-to guy; whatever struggles with world history I have had, he has made infinitely easier, in many untold dimensions. Despite having the run of the house, Nick and Olivia have taken up residence in my study. They are endlessly patient and have tried to give me space while I hashed out drafts of this book. I hope they realize how deeply my world history commitments spring from a desire to anticipate the future of their worlds.

────── How to Make Use of This Book ──────

TO THE HUNDREDS and hundreds of teachers who've thought about and taught world history much longer than I, I salute you. And I offer this primer humbly, in the knowledge that the more world history you know, the more you realize the less you know. I suppose that is true of all histories, but the challenges of any world history project seem infinitely — nay, impossibly — magnified. I don't pretend to be anything like an expert in the field, or to have the most comprehensive view of the many possibilities of how best to teach global pasts in all their complexity. Nor am I equipped to provide examples that span all places and times, or engage every single method or genre in the field. Like most everyone who approaches the task of designing and teaching entry-level world history, I have specific training as a historian that has been supplemented over the years, mainly piecemeal, by new knowledge bases and competencies. And my experiences and convictions have been shaped by the fact that in the public university where I teach I am locked into a large, 150- to 225-student lecture course version of world history, which places constraints on all kinds of things, not least the textbooks I use and the forms of one-to-one proactive learning I can undertake in the space of the classroom itself.

My limits are, in fact, legion. I draw mainly on post-1300 events and processes. As a British-empire historian, I have expertise in South Asian history and some knowledge of African history; as a feminist historian, I have expertise in women, gender, and sexuality, which, with the body, I use as a method for getting at a variety of histories. I am a cultural historian by intellectual and political disposition, but I am also interested in grand narrative, its power and limitations. And last but not least, I recognize that I imagine world history from a very particular locative position, that of the United States, and that the imprint of that location is profound and likely inescapable despite my attempts to unsettle it. I hope you will read this book not as a declaration of what world history teaching ought to be, but as a version of what it might be, or at least as a catalyst for thinking about what your version—or versions—could be.

I've laid out ten design principles, but they are emphatically not *the* ten design principles by which one could construct and execute a world history syllabus. Each chapter is written to be self-contained, so you need not read in order. This is not a textbook; it's a workbook, an aid to figuring out how to design your syllabus around key principles and implement that syllabus in a classroom setting. The emphasis on design is to encourage you to think about how to plan your course when faced with such a vast array of possible subjects, methods, themes, timeframes, and evidence. The design emphasis will also, I hope, encourage you to think about your syllabus as an argument for the urgency of sedimenting protocols of historical thinking and analysis at the heart of discussions about the global. My approach is necessarily schematic, and I fully expect each reader to argue with my choice of principle or example every step of the way. The book itself is the product of just such arguments with colleagues and students and friends. Though I have included some suggestions—for reading, for evidence, for method—from readers that I have not myself used, my examples are mainly ones that I have worked with. I am sure they look narrow and naïve to people who have expertise in the specific arenas I've chosen or who have taught for so long that they have a far deeper bench of reference materials than I. I've been frank about what I do and don't do in the classroom, but only suggestively, not prescriptively, I hope. What works for me may not for you; and, as is often the case, what works in one semester for me may not even work as well the next. As I've confessed at various places in the text, I have not worked out everything in my own syllabus or lectures to my satisfaction, not by any means. I still struggle with how best to address certain questions, engage the empirical and the conceptual, and help students acquire both short-term knowledge and long-term skills. For better or worse, the struggle is the thing—that dynamic, contingent thing that keeps historians thinking, arguing, writing, and revising stories large and small. And for better or worse, it's never done. So please accept what follows as principled but provisional—like all critically engaged history, in short.

A Primer for Teaching World History

Why Design?

THINKING THROUGH WORLD HISTORY 101

Primer, n.: a handbook of fundamental principles.
Primer, n.: a flat coat: the first or preliminary layer of
paint applied to prepare a surface.
Primer, n.: a cap or chamber that supplies compound for
igniting a charge of powder; a catalyst.

THE CASE FOR TEACHING world history has arguably
been made, but best practices for making it work in a classroom setting are by no means self-evident. This book is intended as a companion for teachers who may be designing an
introductory-level world history syllabus for the first time; for
those who already teach world history and are seeking new
ideas or approaches; and for those who train future teachers
in the art of preparing a course in any historical subject with a
global or transnational focus. Art and design in a history syllabus may strike you as unrealistic at worst, fanciful at best.
And yet without design principles and your distinctive imprint, a syllabus — the term derives from a Greek word mean-

ing papyrus roll—will simply be a statement of content about readings and lectures, rather than a living, dynamic account of your vision of what "world history" can or should be. One of the chief goals of this book is to encourage teachers to think about the world history syllabus as having an architecture—a fundamental, underlying structural design that shapes students' experiences, offers pathways into and out of "the global," and, above all, leaves students with a skill set for apprehending the world, past and present, that is adaptable to both their larger pursuit of study and their lives as twenty-first-century citizens. It's a design upon which you leave your mark, even as you engage evidence and methods that may be drawn from diverse and often competing frames of reference and analysis. Your world history syllabus is, in other words, an interpretive device of your own making—a kind of GPS—and as such it bears the marks of your convictions about the work of "history" and "worldliness" in the classroom and beyond.

Though most of us who teach history do so out of a baseline conviction about why it's an important subject, it's worth reconnecting with those first principles as you begin your syllabus design. For one thing, involving students in the nitty-gritty of historical thinking and historical method should be a consistent and purposeful feature of your course planning. You can't do that effectively if the rationales for taking an introductory-level history course—for itself, and as opposed to anthropological or sociological approaches to the global—aren't on the tip of your tongue or at the front end of your process. As we shall see, conversations about "why history?" can and should be a regular component of the course, an active ingredient of assignments as well as lecture and discussion content.

For me, history is indispensable because it reminds us of the contingency of time and place for so many concepts, phenomena, and experiences: democracy, slavery, childbearing, violence, patriotism, credit, mobility, and even history itself. Knowing about the past means having access to models and countermodels of political organization, social power, economic change, and cultural encounter. The study of history also allows for genealogy, the process of tracking who "we" are and how we got to where we are now. History is also, perforce, interdisciplinary. Historians draw on a variety of methods they have borrowed from anthropology, literary criticism, geography, and sociology to answer questions about the past. In an era when history may look ever more traditional — in part because of the accelerating pace of the global and its corollary, perpetual newness — being clear in the syllabus design and throughout the course about why history is an invaluable tool for grappling with all manner of problems and questions is crucial to introductory world history. A set of convictions about how history equips us to think, weigh evidence, and make judgments is, in other words, an integral part of how we teach. Such convictions are equally critical to how we test, which is why structurally centering your commitment to a historical method, or perhaps to multiple methods, in the syllabus and making that commitment part of your daily course discussion can make all the difference to students, especially in an introductory-level class.

Far more challenging for many of us, I think, is defining what we intend when we invite students into the arena of world history. If you've shopped even casually for a world history textbook, you may feel like the narrator in Ted Kooser's poem, "On the Road": you casually pick up a pebble, get a glimpse of the "grand explanation" it contains, drop the pebble, and keep on walking.[1] If you've headed down the textbook road even a little, you know how intimidating it can be, and that there are as many approaches as there are editorial teams and websites. This primer is emphatically not a guide to those resources, which are vast and, like the Googlesphere itself, seem to be multiplying at an exponential rate. You will find a select bibliography at the end of this book, and I will refer on occasion to specific texts, cases, methods, and philosophies. Because I have designed an introductory world history course in several iterations over the last twenty years, I am already committed to a set of principles, an architecture, for my course that I will elaborate below. But I am not invested in determining which approach you choose. I suggest instead that you choose an approach or a mix of approaches, install them at the heart of your syllabus — your particular map of world history — and be prepared to think through, as well as talk through, those choices as the course unfolds. This decision-making is up to you; the design-making is what is important here, because pro-active design is the building block of the course itself and, in turn, the gateway to students' experience of it. My premise is that you need to think about your design principles from the get-go, as part of your lesson plan for the class, and return to them whenever and wherever they crop up so that students get more than a glimpse of your aspirations for the course and for them.

So, for example, you might be committed to the global via a focus on big processes, or to comparison between ecumenes or civilizations or eras. You may be interested in spinning your world history course on the pivot of the environment, on cultural encounters, on trade and economic exchange, on units of space organized by ocean currents, or on slices of time framed by cataclysmic events, natural or human-made. You might even build your course on a series of biographies — women and men who made the world. There are textbooks and myriad other resources for each of these approaches. These approaches, and many others besides, are all, in theory, open to you. And that is one reason world history is so intimidating to newcomers and veterans alike. With the exception of the most recent PhDs coming out of a handful of institutionalized world history programs, very few of us have been trained in world history per se. Most of us are struggling to learn vast new swaths of history: we are moving beyond our comfort zones into new primary sources, new bodies of evidence, even new concepts (like the transnational, the interregional, the epochal, and my personal favorite, the "transversal"). And depending on our conditions of work, we are doing so quickly, under pressures of various sorts, in the context of large numbers of students and outcome-oriented curricula, and with varying abilities to choose the tools we have at our disposal or the kinds of tests we administer. An emphasis on design and its principles suggests that one way to navigate the vastness of time, place, and topic that presents itself to anyone taking up the teaching of world history is to identify an interpretive focus and stick with it, to choose narratives and primary sources that tack to that focus. This focus lends coherence to the course, giving you a framework on which to hang examples, narratives, arguments and exercises. An interpretive focus enables you to begin to control the potentially limitless amount of information that is available to you but would take lifetimes to access, let alone master.

Deciding on a set of design principles means conceding that you are not after "coverage" in a conventional sense but are choosing specific filters through which students are enabled to make historical knowledge and interpretations for themselves, with your help. It also signals a rejection of haphazard or, worse, "cafeteria" coverage: if it's Tuesday, it must be the Silk Road. Ideally, your decision means that you are telescoping your syllabus, focusing in on a particular set of commitments (including timeframe and themes) that are articulated at the start, are threaded through the course as a whole, and are tested for along the way. It means identifying — for yourself and for your students — what you want students to learn about history and "the world" from the outset and making those claims the centerpiece of your plan for the course. One educator has called this a process of deciding "what skein of implications and affiliations and hints and directions" you plan to weave.[2] In any case, you are not historicizing the planet, you are making an informed set of choices about, and constructing a justifiably targeted view of, world history, itself a contested concept and a vibrant field in the making. You are, in short, aiming to show what history looks like, how it works in "the grip of worldly encounter."[3] Such a principled posture can generate a lot of intellectual and pedagogical energy, which is exhilarating even and especially inside a robust design frame.

At first glance, the call for design principles — what we might call a spine for the syllabus — may appear constraining. Why would you want to sew everything up around one approach or method from the start? Isn't the messiness, the unevenness of history, precisely what a global dimension can capture? And how can one approach do justice to the multiply moving parts of the forces of world history over time and space? Each of these challenges has merit and each merits a response. In identifying your design principles you need not choose one; it's not necessary to cut the whole cloth with one repetitive stroke. You might break your syllabus into three consecutive parts and choose approaches that best suit the timeframes and themes under consideration. And in fact, it's probably true that the best syllabi are built over time, with frames of analyses emerging organically from the bottom up, rather than from the top down. It may take two or three iterations of the course to feel comfortable enough to even think about implementing a recurrent design. It took me many years of tinkering and rethinking to get where I am now with my syllabus, and even so it never feels done.[4] But if you do decide to impose one or two overarching principles at the start, you need not do so slavishly or mono-lithically. Part of your project might be to make a case for the viability of civilizational comparisons, for example, in the premodern, non-nation-state world, and to query the use of those comparisons in later periods. Or you might begin with an ocean-oriented approach and float, as it were, in and out of that paradigm as the events or historical forces you want to address warrant. Design principles are meant to be challenged; they are as useful as provocations when they don't work and when they do. If the course has a spine, a central, framing design, that spine is there in part to be held up as such, to be elaborated upon and examined, to be questioned and sometimes even rejected as part of the complex of deliberative think-ing, reading, and writing that all good history courses make available.

And should you end up totally rejecting such a designed approach, you might ask yourself: What are the values and presumptions that emerge from the version of world history I have now created or want to create? What, indeed, are the choices I have made that have become so natural to me that I don't necessarily recognize them as choices?[5] Such presumptions and investments are surely there, though they may be unacknowledged or underacknowledged. What, in effect, is the story I wish to be heard? Is the design of my course enabling that story and its counterhistories? Is my course design developing skills that students can name as historical in a global frame at the end of the class? Will they see the "globalness" of his-tory, as I have modeled it, as an indispensable part of their liberal arts edu-cation toolkit? Is the course design flexible, portable, adaptable to other times and places? And when it is not, can students appreciate why?

Syllabus design is usually pragmatic. It can be idealistic, and it's always strategic, whether we recognize it or not. Like any other apparatus, the syllabus arranges things, and, if we work it right, it can also explain how things are arranged. Much like the introductory lecture in many disciplines, it's a mix of idealism and practicality aimed at engaging students via broad swaths of knowledge and conveying a passion for the subject at hand.[6] More than perhaps we are comfortable admitting, many of us prefer not to think about course design or to leave it to someone else — the textbook writers, the primary-source readers, those in charge of the broader curriculum in our workplace. Others of us are happy to know the design and not reveal it, or to do so at strategic moments, part of the enthralling power of teaching in whatever subject or field. In this primer, I make the case for the use-value of transparent design principles for an introductory world history class not over course content, but in the service of making that content valuable *and* potentially paradigmatic of how power works in certain circumstances, of how subjects act in specific contexts, when global processes are at work and when they are not. Ideally, there will be moments in a world history course when students have a chance to witness the limits of a global analysis and, of course, the limits of historical method. I operate from the conviction that these moments should not be random, as when one throws darts at a board to see what sticks — at least not all of those moments should be random, for some of those darts will ricochet off the wall and right back at you when you have not in the least anticipated them. But I believe that defining and then pressing up against the boundaries of the terrain we identify as world history stretches its capacity as a field and as a carrier of disciplinary method, even as world history pushes us to imagine more capacious and more refined definitions of what it means to be a student of as enlarged a past as we are capable of imagining.

All of this might well be said of any history syllabus; each one surely needs planning, purpose, and intellectual and pedagogical commitments at its structural heart. Why should an introduction to world history command attention to principles of design, method, and strategy? The answer has to do with world history's own curricular trajectory. While the subject has been a staple in a number of tertiary institutions in the United States for the better part of the last three decades, it is only now arriving, often with a vengeance, in colleges and universities where the study of Western civilization may have been the norm. In their capacity as classroom teachers, and often through reorientations of their own research in the context of globalization, historians are looking to repurpose and transform their civilization courses to fit a globalizing curriculum (or to act as a gadfly on that curriculum). These shifts often entail refashioning or overhauling a rise-and-fall civilizational model that privileged Western arcs and events and narratives even when that model was, in a real sense, transnational by virtue of being trans-European, intercontinental, or both. The demand at the secondary level in the United States is even greater. Sixty percent of states currently require a world history course for graduation, and the World History AP test is the seventh most popular administered by the College Board. With world history teaching fast becoming a linchpin at all levels of curricular development, there is a rush to fill the perceived gap in pedagogical resources, training materials, and instructional modules so that students and teachers alike can catch up — and can demonstrate competency in a subject with "practical" application in a globalizing world.

In the face of this palpable urgency about the need to teach more world history, the question of what kind of world history we teach has never been more pressing. We are presumably resistant to the "content farm" model of education in which students troll for information on the global in response to a market-driven view of learning. And we certainly don't want design to become such a preoccupation that it "all but replaces" the substance of what we teach.[7] And yet the pressure of the present, when globalization seems naturalized and without a history — the logical outcome of apparently teleological forces moving from the West to "the rest" — makes the stakes for a principled, design-driven syllabus perhaps unprecedentedly high. Was today's globalization inevitable? Is it only the most recent in successive waves of globalization? Is globalization a codeword for historical processes — capitalism, empire, Western "civilization," and Americanization? Are our models for globality only to be found in the context of Western modernity? How do we assess, compare, and juxtapose "big" historical events over time and space? What counts as big? Is the local a thing of the past? What did the world look like to people a thousand years ago, and where did they see the world from, when and if they saw it?

In part because the stakes are so high, this primer is motivated by my conviction that how we do world history is as important as that we do it, if not more so. We should be conscious of our principles, and design our courses, train future teachers, and challenge contemporary students accordingly. We ought to be able to name our structural approaches, defend our pedagogical choices, and admit the limits of those choices in the face of all comers, modeling an ambition for world history and a humility about its total explanatory power. This is, arguably, one formula for compelling and enduring history of all kinds. And we ought to be able to convey to students that academic learning "is but one model of intellectual life," and but one pathway to a lifelong love of learning, including a love of history.[8] I hope this book will do what all primers should do, in theory and in practice: serve as an elementary text, apply a first coat for others to paint over, and catalyze critical thinking about what kind of world histories we want to think with, learn from, undo, and recreate as we go.

— PART I —

Laying Foundations

IN PART I of the primer, I lay out some of the organizing principles and commitments that might animate your syllabus. In schematic terms, the chapters cover time, space, and scale by addressing where to start, how to think about connections, why women and the body are critical concepts, and how attention to histories from below might enable you to think broadly about the global. While PART I offers specific historical *examples* to illustrate each case, *strategies* that will help you with lectures and discussions are found in PART II.

Chapter One

Timing

WHEN TO START

DECIDING WHICH SLICE or slices of time to cover in a world history course is one of the most daunting hurdles for someone designing an introductory-level syllabus under that rubric. Ideally your syllabus should bracket off a targeted period with specific dates (for example, 1450–1900 or 800–1492), but it can also identify a beginning point, with the promise of ending in the contemporary moment, a moment broadly or narrowly conceived (for example, 1350–present or 1850–2012). Either way, your chronological markers should do more than delimit decades or swaths of time. Nor should they simply sit in the second half of your course title, the results of a quick decision or the products of available textbooks and source readers. They should serve as orientation devices, allowing students to follow a temporal blueprint that you have designed out of a commitment to tracking specific timeframes, whether epic or quotidian. And chronological markers should act as recurrent pedagogical reference points as the course unfolds, drawing students' attention back to the specific moment in time for all events, ideas, movements, politics, economic developments, and encounters you would have students engage. The dates you choose should, in other words, underscore on a regular basis the temporal contingencies of the histories you are generating—contingencies that mark the global past as much as they do any other history. Chronological markers are foundational, in short, to the architecture of your syllabus. As such, they announce the chronological dimensions of your argument about the scope and scale of world history and provide an opening for sharing your choices and your focus with students.

If you are free to choose your start and end dates, making that choice may seem daunting or vexing. But taking the leap and imposing a temporal frame on the global landscapes that your course animates—thinking about beginning and ending dates—actually takes you to the heart of debates about the when, the where, and the how of world history. In curricula taught in the United States, an obvious point of departure might be 1500—in part because this enables teachers to stage "New World" conquest as a monumental event. That break aligns with older models of medieval, early modern, and modern divisions. Such models can be Eurocentric, but they need not be: "c. 1500" can be a useful pivot point for capturing the simultaneity of the Mughals, the late Ming and the Qing, and (more of a stretch) the Tokugawa era, simultaneous with each other and with the so-called age of discovery. If you are set on a civilizational approach, sometime around 1500 might well suit you. This is especially true if you are willing to view the starting date as somewhat flexible. There's no reason, for example, not to call your course World History from 1500 to the Present, but do an opening session or two on why you chose 1500 as your point of departure and what the world looked like at 1500. One tack is to provide students with a short (or long) genealogy of that moment. Such an exercise might involve using Columbus's "discovery" of the Americas (1492) as a critical antecedent. The Treaty of Tordesillas (1494) might work just as well; so, for that matter, might a focus on Tenochtitlan in the thirteenth century, two centuries before Cortés. If you want the emphasis on temporality to come full circle, you can talk about how excavations near the city site of Tenochtitlan in the 1970s uncovered the

Piedra del Sol (Stone of the Sun), initially believed to be an Aztec calendar. Discussion of the stone's actual function (as an archive of Aztec cosmology) would return you to the history of time measurement before 1500, beyond the West, at the heart of a sophisticated and powerful civilization.[1] In some classrooms, the Piedra del Sol might be mobilized as evidence of "the time of the Other."[2] In other syllabi, it might spark a conversation about contemporary museum display and the reliance of global tourism on the "ruins" of the past. Or a conversation might begin about the sense of difference between us and them that tourism tends to produce.

Before you put your stake in the ground at any particular place, you might want to consider other possibilities for the parameters of your world history syllabus. Work by scholars like Janet Abu-Lughod and Andre Gunder Frank, for example, suggests that there is good reason to push the start date back a few hundred years before 1500, in order to get outside the New World–Old World dyad and to think about the premodern world as multiaxial — to think about it more precisely as global, rather than as operating from the presumption that the modern and the global are necessarily synonymous or in lockstep.[3] Here the example of Afro-Eurasia — a hyphenated name that scholars like Gunder Frank have suggested captures the intercontinental world of trade and exchange that characterized the fourteenth century and the fifteenth — works well as a spatial device because it dramatizes a very specific moment in "global" time when these regions were interlocked, if not also mutually constitutive. Although this may sound self-evident, students need examples big and small to help them appreciate why such regional formations are contingent on a specific timeframe. Afro-Eurasia is a good example, in part because it was not transhistorical: it animated worldly processes and was animated by them at a specific conjuncture. It models, as well, one form that the global took in world history before modern times. As an example of premodern globality, Afro-Eurasia is priceless because it puts paid to the notion that contemporary manifestations of globalization are new in historical terms. Tuning out the mantra of the newness of globalization is hard enough for scholars of all stripes to do; a world history course that is conscious, even hyperconscious, of the uneven, unpredictable time of global histories has the potential to equip students with evidence that challenges the presumptive equations we often hear in the media and even in other disciplines. What's more, inviting students to see different historical forms of global processes or interactions challenges the assumption that globalization is above or outside history. It can also reveal how, when, and under what conditions the global is fitful or incomplete, which may in turn lead to a more critical appreciation of the inevitability, or not, of today's global systems.

There are several ways to drive home these points about early examples of what might be termed global or globalizing forces, trends, and phenomena. One is to challenge the putative insularity of Europe before Columbus, not simply by rehearsing examples of trade and encounter but by mapping the inflow and outflow of goods and travelers across multiple borders in ways that illuminate what a premodern world system looked like. I like to use the Champagne fairs, which were vibrant, global marketplaces in action, bringing silk from faraway China, leather from neighboring Italy, and a system of credit and debit that linked the emergence of global capitalism to the rhythms of the liturgical calendar. Not only that, the profits from the fairs lined the coffers of all kinds of people, middling to noble. In my course, I linger on the figure of Blanche of Navarre, countess of Champagne, whose fair income went to building almshouses for the poor and to financing the Crusades. If they had a visual image of Christendom, her "locals" may have understood that a place like the Levant was in their spiritual and even commercial orbit. Navarre's patronage of "locals" might have helped to make concrete their sense of themselves as part of complex of systems beyond their immediate ken: they would have had visible proof of the impact of international credit in their midst — and of the link between their market and the defense of Christendom writ large, as well. Such entanglements are evidence of the continual traffic between "East" and "West" and the challenges of holding fast to those geographical distinctions.[4] And as a late medieval phenomenon whose global outcroppings and returns can be seen and felt well beyond their specific or even extended moment in time, the Champagne fairs delimit a very specific circuitry that may be differently global than, say, Walmart, but which nonetheless offers an early model of a global form that students may have imagined originated much closer to their own lifetimes.

Another tack for starting the time of the global before "modernity" is to move beyond the shores of Europe altogether. Here the maritime empire of China is especially powerful, not least because it dramatizes the precariousness of claims about the centrality of Europe to early world systems. Historians have argued that "Asia" was itself a world system — with strong regional economies, extension into Southeast Asia, and links to European empires and the Americas though silver and crops like maize. An effective way of conveying the scope and reach of China in the premodern world economy is via the figure of Zheng He (1371–1435), a navigator of the period who is a common staple of primary-source books because of his many long-distance voyages and their capacity, in turn, to map a web of Sino-centered systems. That he anticipated Columbus and was, broadly speaking, a contemporary of Marco Polo means that Zheng He can function as a pivotal figure in a syllabus that seeks to complicate conventional chronologies — a syllabus that tries to explicate those chronologies through familiar and unfamiliar individuals. If we were to take the arguments about the Sinocentrism of this period seriously, we might shape an entire world history syllabus that put Asia at the center of the course, using either a 1500–present designation or a completely different set of markers that speak more purposefully to that orientation.

Even allowing for the possibility that some readers of this primer may have been trained in East Asian history, it's possible that some, if not many, of you would feel unequipped to conduct a world history course from the vantage point of China; such a maneuver may be beyond your training or otherwise beyond your scope. You might feel more ready to think about making China "central" by following the mobility of Chinese laborers and merchants across world systems: a kind of moving-subject approach that allows you to wend your way across all kinds of temporal and spatial divides and track China's longstanding global impacts in the process.[5] And yet, even if you go with a conventional periodization, making note at the end of a Columbus lecture, for example, that such earlier histories exist, and throw the significance of Columbus's much-heralded discovery into bold relief, this already opens up alternate temporal pathways. Indeed, even as a passing reference, such a remark or set of allusions makes clear the stake in the ground you have made, a stake that forecloses other timeframes and vantage points in the past. For students in the United States especially, this is a way of asking them to account for the time-frames they take for granted, those that never occurred to them, and those around which your account of world history is organized. U.S.-based students can also profitably be encouraged to account for why they take certain timeframes for granted. That "why" includes the limits of your own training and current knowledge, of course. It draws a bright line between "beginnings" and spatial orientation, reminding both you and your students that when you start shapes where you start, and vice versa. And in the best possible world, it acts as a bookmark for you, flagging future reading and the possibility that the next time you do the course you will give more space to what is currently outside your chosen temporal frame or current historiographical knowledge base. For the purposes of thinking Sinocentrism comparatively, one citation might be Suraiya Faroqhi's *The Ottoman Empire and the World Around It*, which makes the case for the world-system character of the sixteenth-century and seventeenth-century Ottoman worlds.[6]

There are, needless to say, a variety of more dramatic ways to take different temporalities seriously. Working expressly from an economic model, rather than from a political or cultural model, is deracinating in the best sense, because it marks time through commerce and trade, potentially making "weights, measures, value, means of payment and contracts" your units of analysis—and dramatizing how their meanings and functions have fluctuated over time.[7] In keeping with this emphasis on the economic, silver is the best friend a world history teacher can have: China's move from paper and copper currency to silver in the fifteenth century was the fiscal equivalent of the shot heard round the world, drawing multiple polities into a world economy for the next two centuries at least. Beyond silver per se, and as Kenneth Pomeranz and Steven Topik have shown, centering economic histories allows you to foreground market conventions, transportation networks, and the "economics of violence" as genuinely global processes that both mimic conventional chronologies and cut across them.[8] Especially if your focus is "first globalizations," this allows you to explore moments in time when something "other than commodity exchange might, in fact, have comprised (and in the future, might again comprise) 'the normal functioning of the market.'"[9] The view from "economic time" is disorienting and reorienting at once.

Cutting loose from civilizational models and working through units defined by shared belief systems (Christendom), economic processes (the Silk Road), or littorals (like those across the Indian Ocean world) is another way to go. This kind of regional or transregional approach can structure the whole course or can be used at strategic moments to complicate a familiar and fairly linear narrative. I am thinking here of how some scholars have used the framework of the Atlantic world to give new dimensions to the "triangular" slave trade, and vice versa. Centering environmental or climatological histories has the potential for creating whole new chronologies organized around tectonic shifts, zoological transformations, and epidemiological upheavals. The "global intensification of land use" alone could serve as the basis for a sweeping yet grounded global history.[10] Similarly, a world history course that takes oceans and oceanic regions as its basis could capture the global from a whole new set of angles, and might work from the premise that eons of time are the best units of analysis, rather than comparatively shorter intervals — or it could make 1450–1950 look like a short interval, comparatively speaking.[11] Indeed, cutting across big scales of time to see both shared characteristics of polity, economy, and process *and* to evaluate what a compressed view of time (one century, two) might do to our claims about change or stasis is one way to approach your study of the world. What difference does it make to our understandings of the global to note, for example, that carbon consumption and emission grew exponentially in the comparatively short time span of the industrial revolution and its aftermath? And what difference does it make that such patterns were uneven globally as "the North" and "the West" extracted resources from "the South" and "the East," even as demographics show tremendous migration flows along those same pathways? Slicing the world map with wide swaths of time allows big trends to emerge, offering a planetary view that diminishes human history — by placing it in environmental context — in ways that are worthy of long and compelling discussion.

This is the kind of argument put forward by David Christian in his book *Maps of Time: An Introduction to Big History*, in which time is measured in millennia and world zones emerge in the context if epic cycles.[12] There are a number of advantages to this kind of approach. As I have suggested, it has the capacity to center the environment, both terrestrial and celestial, and to contextualize, even provincialize, human history in relationship to it. Such an approach doesn't presuppose civilizations or nation-states or empires as the foundational units of either historical experience or historical analysis; and because it privileges "thinking the world" in the broadest terms possible, it has the capacity to cultivate connections between facts and "broader patterns and generalizations" — skills we all want students to have. So committed are Christian and others to this "big era" method, they have modeled it out as a total curricular project via UCLA's National Center for History in the Schools under the title "A Compact History of Humankind for Teachers and Students."[13]

Significantly, this model does not cede the floor to claims that "history becomes vacuous at large scales." And yet, like many of us who approach world history in the classroom, big history proponents are also concerned with organizing the subject in "manageable pieces." As a general principle, and as this chapter has endeavored to show, "manageability" is a perfectly respectable objective when contemplating the chronological ambit of your syllabus, not least because it's part of the partial view of the world you have self-consciously staked out in your course. To that I would add manageability with a purposeful syllabus design that helps to structure the arguments — thematic, evidentiary, methodological — of the whole course. So if you choose to stage your world history course from 800– 1450, you should think about what that frame buys and how you plan to carry through with its promise from lecture to lecture, session to session, assignment to assignment. Are these high political markers? Do they run a line only between "major events," or can they be used to touch down in daily life or among ordinary histories as well? Elsewhere, dates might bracket histories that have no standard chronology; those dates may be a first stab at periodizing a global history that has no comprehensive text or extended narrative, as yet. So, a syllabus pivoting global history on indigenous communities might run 1280–1980, beginning with the date of the first archaeological evidence of Maori in New Zealand, moving through Great Plains history to Ainu peoples under the Meiji Restoration, and ending with tribal peoples' anti-dam protests on the threshold of neoliberalization in India. Or, taking a cue from Ben Kiernan's book *Blood and Soil: A World History of Genocide and Extermination from Sparta to Darfur*, you could approach world history through genocide, offering a deep genealogy of the twentieth-century European holocaust, pivoting backwards in time from midcentury Germany, or even further forward and backward, from Sparta to Darfur, as Kiernan's subtitle suggests.[14] The possibilities are endless — dizzyingly so — and these are admittedly sweeping, almost breathless alternatives to the "Plato to NATO" model of civilizational and global time. If these alternatives were fleshed out, they would need to be grounded in discrete, historically specific examples, examples that create events with connective tissue and demonstrate divergence and difference in time. Your syllabus should make a coherent and persistent case for *when* the worldliness of world history is visible, *when* it recedes, *when* it is thwarted, *when* it returns, and under what conditions it does, when and if it does.

Chances are you don't have as much creative latitude as you would like; chances are you are teaching world history in an already established curriculum, under conditions not fully of your making. You may not even have the opportunity to choose your own textbook or other materials. What do you do then? Even if you are locked into a textbook with a well laid out time line, you can still leave your mark. How you decide to break down the big picture is crucial to how students come away understanding world history. One option is to give your syllabus well signposted subsections. If you have a semester-long course, three subsections will usually suffice after one or two introductory lessons (and allowing for any in-class tests and a final exam). Your sections may reflect forward motion — "Conquest and

Interdependence to 1700," or "Global Economies and Uneven Developments from 1900" — or they may capture an era in a transnational frame,
such as with the title "Age of Revolutions" or "Global Cold Wars." Beyond
these rubrics, framing your students' understandings of the global inside
these broad temporal strokes is a huge challenge. But you can build arguments rooted in specific times and places inside each section, so that your
particular lectures, discussions, and class sections help to make the case of
the subsection. Though it is all but a cliché, I've found that treating the
age of late eighteenth century revolutions — American, French, Haitian,
and Latin American — prismatically, as part of an intellectual, political,
and economic ecumene that spanned 1750–1820, advances a definition of
"global" that insists on temporal specificity even as it allows for an elon-
gated view of "age" or "era." "Age of Revolutions" could be the title of one
of your three syllabus subsections, and the subsection could even include
the industrial revolution, whether tracked in the aforementioned places
or ranged alongside them, with their relationships to one another worked
out more or less in lecture and discussion, depending on what your short-
term goals for the section and your long-term goals for the syllabus are.
As I will discuss in greater length in chapter 10, "Testing (for) the Global,"
quizzes, exams, and assignments tailored to these goals consolidate the
pedagogical processes you've been working to implement and can help to
guarantee that students come away with a sense of the import of change
over time, simultaneities of events and experiences, and temporal disjunctures and disruptions.

I've spent the bulk of this chapter on where to start your world history
story. Where you end it is as important, for it signals to students what the
chronological arcs are for the themes and ideas you have embedded in the
syllabus. There are as many endpoints as there are points of departure and,
as the twenty-first century begins to throw the twentieth into bolder relief for those who were born into the twentieth century and came of age
in it, where to finish can be bedeviling. High school and college students,
even those who are nontraditional, are increasingly born in the new century, or to have little living memory of the most recent fin de siècle. So if
you cast your syllabus as a 1350-present, 1500-present, or something akin

to that, I urge you to take the pressure of the contemporary moment into account whenever you can. I begin my own world history course in part with a story of how I got to be at the front of a world history classroom. I talk about my father, using images of him as a soldier in the Second World War and rehearsing his war experience, his route to college via the GI bill, and the various ways that my own biography is a result of a collision with world-history forces that grew out of his locations in history. I also speak of my mother's immigrant family experiences, and of their imprint on my various trajectories. Had my father been killed in the war, had my Italian grandmother's family business not burned down in Argentina, I wouldn't be here.

Though I haven't yet tried it, I have considered diagramming those stories — creating chains and webs of connection between my biography and recognizably historical events on the blackboard or in an overhead — to help students visualize the global pathways that have eventuated in the interpretive frameworks of their syllabus, however indirectly.[15] I would then ask students to do the same for their own "personal" global histories. To situate themselves in historical time in such a performative way, however, is not to make history subjective. It is to remind them that, as Daniel Segal has observed, "all of human existence, and not just a privileged subset of it, must be treated as historical, in the important senses of involving both contingency and agency, and requiring, on our part as historians, attention to context."[16] Like many of us who seek to engage students in the art of historical thinking, I encourage students from the get-go to consider themselves as historical subjects, as the products of encounters with world-history forces — whether local, global, regional, national, or transnational — within a specific set of times and places. If they leave the first day of their intro-level world history class primed to appreciate the pressure of historical time on their own histories, then we've found a place to begin, and to build off as well.

Chapter Two

Centering Connectivity

AS A SUBJECT, as a method, and as an interdiscipline, world history is nothing if not diverse. It's no exaggeration to say that there are as many approaches to teaching "globally" as there are textbooks. Primary-source readers, which also abound, act as orientation devices, shaping the chronological arcs and thematic investments of syllabi in entry-level courses and beyond. Assessing the field in 2003, Patrick Manning lamented that in the wake of accelerating attention to world history as a teaching field in the 1990s, publishers rushed to fill the marketplace with series and course materials with such blind ambition that the result was a bit of a "grab bag" for would-be teachers: so much to choose from, so few navigational tools.[1] As Manning has also observed, organizations of professional historians in the United States, like the American Historical Association, have taken world history seriously in the last two decades, publishing pamphlets, sponsoring workshops and plenary sessions, and pursuing a variety of experiments, digital and otherwise, to bring the tenets of historical inquiry to bear on global phenomena and to ask how the protocols of history might change under the pressure of such objects of inquiry. The growth and development of the World History Association with a host of new journals and electronic fora in this same period, means that world history is big business, in publishing, in curriculum planning at all levels, and as part of the global citizenship profile of institutions of higher education both inside and outside North America.

The emergence of both a College Board AP course in the subject and required courses in states with some of the biggest populations in the United States during this same period makes world history teaching more than a trend: it's part of a national curriculum that aims to deliver a variety of world history knowledge to students of all ages — a hot-button political issue at least since the second Bush administration, if not before.[2] The fact that the creation of global pasts for Americans is at risk from both the Arizona immigration law (which would exclude undocumented immigrant children from classrooms) and the Texas textbook revisions (which seriously narrow the purview of "American" history) demonstrates that the marketplace of ideas in world history is basically unregulated, offering multiple models of how to engage with multisited stories of the human experience, from the micro to the macro, from the comparative to the transnational, from the local to the intraregional, from the oceanic to the multipolar, to the planetary as well. To echo Martin Heidegger, world history — as a subject and as a field — is so gigantic that we can scarcely see it, scarcely take it all in.[3]

How, then, to materialize the world's histories for students who stand in a very particular place in it and, depending on where they live in the United States, may be tempted to see their world as *the* world, without fully appreciating what's at stake in that perception? And, for that matter, what counts as "the world"? I'd like to nominate connectivity as one design principle, one method for bringing the "world picture" of world history into sharper focus. Though links, bridges, connections, and interdependencies are staples of the world history lexicon, I am struck, as you may be as well, by how little attention is given to the meanings of those terms, to their capacity for actually shaping the direction of a syllabus beyond the opening statement of purpose, let alone their capacity for impacting how the course is broken down or how the student's appreciation of the global is assessed. I embrace connectivity here as a model not because I believe it's the only way to think through an introductory syllabus, but because I've found that as an interpretive grid, connectivity allows teachers and students to plot and critically assess the work of global processes and phenomena in historical context. In that sense, connectivity is not a camera designed to take snapshots of the past; it works more like a search engine designed to follow patterns of circulation and interdependence and evaluate their limits and possibilities.[4] When it's mobilized as a positioning device in a world history syllabus, connectivity offers a way of tracking and measuring—instead of assuming—the "globalness" of a political event, an economic practice, a social movement, or a cultural formation. Like a GPS, connectivity is a navigation system that requires a promontory view, serving as an aid to mapmaking and to students' consciousness of their position in time and space. In that sense, although connectivity encourages students to see the world as a whole, it's equally an attempt to apply a politics of location, and of contingency, to the problem of world history. Rather than cultivating a blind conviction about transhistorical connections—everything is global—connectivity encourages students to ask, following Adrienne Rich: If world history makes the global visible, "where do we see it from, is the question?"[5]

As a design principle, connectivity operates from the presumption that space is as important as time for appreciating the complexities of the past. Drawing on the work of geographers especially, historians interested in the basic subjects of the discipline—change, power, hierarchy, catastrophe, race and gender difference, circulation, political economy, governmentality, militarism, material culture, resistance, identity, trade, the body, sovereignty, mobility, work, and the law—have become spatial thinkers in the last two decades, in ways that have huge payoffs for teaching world history. Richard White's *Middle Ground*—which maps the spaces of encounters between Native Americans and colonizers in the Great Lakes region over a century and half of expansion, resistance, accommodation, and mixture—is emblematic of this spatial turn, as is his Spatial History

Project at Stanford.⁶ As White himself is quick to point out, the spatial turn is not new. Historians across the world, from Herodotus to W. E. B. DuBois to Romila Thapar, have drawn on spatial metaphors or referenced their "home places" with geographical imaginaries that not only crossed borders but rendered them clearly, to us as well as to those who shared their time and place, as functions of specific historical forces, rather than as timeless or permanently true, even if we allow for their military or technological power. More recently, and in the shadow of global capital and its circulatory systems, students of the past are increasingly interested in links between and among apparently discrete spaces, in converse and reverse flows, in localized, interregional circuitry, and, of course, in times and places where communities were not engaged with systems or much beyond their immediate surroundings. Africanists in particular have been skeptical about the application of the global as a universalizing spatial category because of what they know about how continental societies above and below the Sahara operated, the impact of the slave trade notwithstanding.⁷ And as the anthropologist Karen Ho has pointed out, the only people as invested as academicians in the "totality" of the global as a kind of unbroken arc of connectivity are bankers in Wall Street firms.⁸ Building off historical research that both promotes and critiques the capacity of space to help us apprehend the global, my working definition of connectivity is "the dynamic (inter)action of historical spaces." In this formulation, space is not simply a surface traveled across but an active agent in history. Dynamism signals the contingency of space on time. And (inter)action is where contact may occur. When they interact, and even when they don't, historical spaces are dynamic: they generate movement, which can enable literal connections. Connectivity is a dimension of history's power and of its powerful potential.

As an orientation device for syllabus construction and lecture and discussion planning, connectivity has several benefits. First, it presumes no natural or necessary center: it's one pathway out of the dichotomous East-West framework, suggesting discrete links and broader patterns of convergence and divergence that may be generalizable but are always ultimately dependent on examples grounded in a particular time and place, or a set of places. For example, if you want to explore the geopolitics of industrialization — if, in other words, you wanted to make your account of the industrial revolution truly global, rather than rehearse it as the story of Britain's dark, satanic mills or as a tale of technology transfer, West to East — you could use connectivity to talk about commodity chains from Bengal to Baton Rouge, or from South America to the heart of the North American prairie, especially if that prairie is conceived as a grasslands biome, stretching from southern Texas to Alberta, and especially if you want to remind students that the industrial revolution by no means displaced agricultural production worldwide. If you want to be less territorial, more littoral, you could use the slave ship and an ocean ecumene as a way into discussions of circulation and mobility, in human and commodity terms. It's also possible, and even highly effective, to begin in one place and think outward from that place to a wider world of travel, trade, and exchange. Caravanserais (roadside inns that served as nodal points for Eurasian trade) work well in this regard, especially if you are interested in material culture or if architecture is a subtheme. Not only do the caravanserais open up pathways, literally and figuratively, into a form of global system that predates the modern period, the visual images, and in some cases the extant examples of caravanserais, literally bear the imprint, aesthetically and in linguistic terms, of the connectivity they sponsored.

Second, and as is implied in much of the above, connectivity allows you to address, frankly and directly, the reciprocity — and the slippage — between the local and the global, especially when you consistently emphasize the question of location, the "where do we see it from?" question. As all world history teachers know, maps are indispensable to this task. They underscore how and why "the world" is a social concept; they literally orient the viewer, sometimes revealing her unexamined orientation to the world in the process. Maps allow for connections — whether measured by proximity or proportion — to be materialized and spaces in between to be understood as historically specific. Screening the frontispiece to the Codex Fejérváry-Mayer (1400–1521), Mercator's projection (c. 1900), and the Peters world map (2004) in succession nicely dramatizes the central premise of connectivity as a design principle, the dynamism of histori-

cal space, and its contingency on the location of the viewer, whether that
location is individual, civilizational, or involves the conjuncture of spaces.[9]
In the case of precolonial India, for example, Sanjay Subrahmanyam asks
why we should think of early modern India as apart from the rest of the
world. Was Bengal any less connected to coastal Burma and Thailand
than Gujarat? Such a skepticism about given borders or established, naturalized, locative positions means, in Subrahmanyam's view, that "we are
obliged more or less constantly to rethink our notions of frontiers and circuits, to redraw maps that emerge from the problematics we wish to study
rather than invent problematics to fit our pre-existent cartographies."[10]
Like alternative chronologies, such revised and perpetually shifting terrains are argumentative, in the sense that they posit a case for unlooked
for *connective* histories — raising critical questions about what counts as
a legitimate space for historical inquiry beyond conventional boundary
markers like state and nation.

Third, connectivity offers a way to track and test the reach of the
global. When connections are tight or regular across space and time, we
have an opportunity to see global connections in action; when they are
not, we have the chance to see the very real power of borders, their capacity to block circulation or mobility — and the comparative isolation
of some populations from the world as well. Indeed, connectivity is not
always conductivity; to appreciate what the global is and is not, what enables claims to the totality of the global and what might put a break on
those claims, students need to witness radical disconnection or partial disjunctures, as well as, and in contrast to, interconnectedness per se. These
disjunctures are what the anthropologist Anna Tsing calls the "sticky en-
gagements" global or semiglobal processes entail.[11] Another kind of dis-
juncture can be found in Donald Wright's *The World in a Very Small Place
in Africa*, which I have either used wholesale or have excerpted in my syllabus. Wright's study of agricultural communities in Niumi, the Gambia,
over the course of several hundred years plots what might be called non-
connectivity. Using the periodization modeled by world systems theory,
Wright shows how comparatively insouciant African farmers entered the
global marketplace, carving a distinctive subsistence niche for themselves,

in an global underdevelopment paradigm, and were totally absorbed by the lure and needs of Western markets.[12] This spatial and structural outside-ness is, of course, quite dynamic over time, as Wright carefully shows. This is less a story of resistance to world market governance than it is of a kind of indifference: evidence of vibrant local economies and trans-regional communities that were neither determined by nor relentlessly oriented toward the futurity of the modern global West. Attention to this and other examples like it in lectures and discussions interrupts what can be a tendency — on students' part as well as on our own, if we do not take care — to celebrate connection rather than to see it as a diagnostic tool. Indeed, for some world historians, the progressive integration of systems and processes, of civilizations and ecospheres, has been not just the story of the global but of world history as a method.[13]

"Africa" is a big place and generalizations can be dangerous. A useful counter to Wright's work is Jeremy Prestholdt's *Domesticating the World*, which explores the consumer desires of East Africans for goods that drew them into markets from the United States to India, desires enabled by the commerce energizing vibrant global and interregional port cities, of which the archipelago Zanzibar was a longstanding hub.[14] Juxtaposing these two cases underscores the use-value of connectivity for enabling students to think globally where the global is not given, but complex and even contradictory. Contrary to the way connectedness is used in mathematics, connectivity as I deploy it does not mean "uninterrupted," or "all of a piece." Placing a deliberate, *critical* emphasis on connectivity encourages students to understand the "worldliness" of world history in this way, that is, by taking up a self-consciously diagnostic, even clinical, posture. That posture is not devoid of emotion or engagement; it can allow students and teachers to be agnostic about the predictability of where and when the global might be found, or about the inevitability of one version of it. In that sense, connectivity is both GPS and "app": it can orient the whole syllabus and it can drop down into particular cases or sets of examples in ways that create momentum in the syllabus even as they interrupt students' presumptions about where global histories happened, for whom and to whom they happened, and under what conditions.

31

You are probably wondering why you need connectivity as a design principle. In the first place, doesn't it preclude other approaches or topics? What if there are instances where comparison is really a better tack? What I like about connectivity is that it need not exclude other approaches. You can compare sovereign units — say, the courts of Suleiman and Louis XIV, as I do in chapter 7, "Empire as a Teaching Tool" — by anatomizing their similarities and differences and making any number of points about the role of court culture and the body shaping early modern absolutism across East and West. You can then ask the connective questions: Were there borrowings, mutual influences? How legitimate a historical claim is it to juxtapose two examples that don't overlap very much in temporal terms? Can I make that connective leap myself, and if so, on what empirical grounds? What if I don't want to focus on big events and structures; or, if I want to balance that with embodied experience, daily life, and individual action on the ground? As I have been suggesting, a commitment to connectivity isn't totalizing; at least it doesn't have to be. You can move from a signature global event — such as the First World War — in one class session to a more specific "local" history in the next, or in the same session. And you could cast that individual or smaller-scale story as a marked contrast to the "big" event. But you can also find many ways to drill down to smaller-scale examples that carry, invariably if not inevitably, traces of connectivity. Take as an example the Russian Revolution. You've just done a lecture, or perhaps even several, on the events of 1917 in a global context. You could turn to a case study of sovietization in the aftermath of the war, focusing on women's "liberation" and Islam in Uzbekistan.[15] Connectivity here is between events and across scales; between Moscow and Central Asia; between colonizer and colonized; and along multiple axes — gender, religion, and politics. If you compare and contrast the reforms undertaken by Atatürk in Turkey or the campaigns against the veil by feminists in Cairo during this same interwar period, you will extend further the connective tissue and produce what a collective of feminist historians has recently called "connective comparison" through "multidirectional citation," insofar as you may have begun in Russia but you've moved laterally across time, layering example on example.[16] You've also centered women and the body, a strategy about which I have more to say in the next chapter. It's possible too that you aren't equipped to do a global version of 1917 because your knowledge or your lack of relevant resources to date doesn't allow for that. Taken together, a unit that puts 1917 in Russia proper into conversation with Central Asian history offers a view of transnational cultural politics from more than one location. You may be content to call this global, semiglobal, or none of the above, but in any case you've asked students to do some work to evaluate the scale and meaning of these interactions across spaces they may not have appreciated as contingent, let alone connected.

But couldn't you do all these things I have suggested without connectivity as an organizing principle? Yes, of course you can. Why do you need connectivity? Without it, what would be the principle or set of assumptions around which you would build your case for the "world" in world history? Presumably the links between spaces and times is one principle; possibly a narrative about successive waves of globalization is another. But surely a world history course needs to engage with or produce a story about interactions of a certain scope and scale — as part of if not as the whole of its rationale. Perhaps you team-teach, as Ann B. Waltner and Mary Jo Maynes have been doing for years at the University of Minnesota. Their approach has been to follow discrete modules (Germany, Africa, Latin America, and China) across time, making links and identifying divergences as those modules move across time. As Waltner and Maynes have written, the modules they work with also sediment gender, sexuality, and the family across the course's whole narrative, which, given the way family forms and gender roles were imitated and appropriated as they shaped and were shaped by the dynamic (inter)action of historical spaces, opens up possibilities for connectivity as a design principle for global social and cultural histories as yet fully untold.[17]

My point is this: if you operate from the assumption that you need an intellectual driver, a pedagogical motor purpose, then connectivity, as I have tried to construct it, is flexible enough to serve as a shell, inside which a variety of different methods and approaches can be nested, and the very presumption of a transhistorical global connectivity can be tested as well.

Let me proceed with a very specific example, one based on a case that is readily available in world history textbooks: the Mongols. A broad lecture about the Mongol invasions can emphasize their global character, using maps to dramatize the sheer spatial reach of Genghis Khan's territorial empire and its long-term significance for the making of Eurasia. The role of women, as military figures and dynastic agents, is indispensable to this story and can be easily tacked to claims about the Mongols' far-flung imperium. That lecture can also "drill down" to the ground by talking about the role of horses in the creation of that empire and citing a variety of examples of battles and skirmishes in which the horse, cannily and violently employed, gave the Mongols a strategic advantage. And for comparison's sake, admittedly across time and space but instructively so, there is the parallel of how the Comanche empire in the American West used horses as well—more defensively, and to try to insulate their communities from European political economies, but with similar strategic intention.[18] One way to close out this specific example and return back to the larger narrative (if you wish) is to talk about the fact that what enabled the Mongol empire—conquest by horseback—was less able to sustain it, given the vast distances that the Khanates needed to oversee and the many challenges of travel by horseback.

This example models several things. It takes a common chestnut in world history and maps it out in time and space, offering a specific example of connectivity in action. It gives flesh (in this case, animal flesh!) to the narrative in ways that both ratify it and qualify its generalizations. And it does so by reaching into and beyond one case study to other times and places for comparison and contrast. Students have appreciated this move, though reviewers of the initial drafts of this book were critical of its too broad comparative reach. I use the Mongol-Comanche "connection" not to advance a transhistorical argument about world-making but precisely to underscore the contingency of all big generalizations: to underscore their dependence on historical context. The comparison offers the possibility of connection to another, perhaps more familiar, horseback conqueror, and it has the potential to encourage students to think about the validity of a comparison of the Mongol with the Comanche. It suggests that stories big and small may be "connected," but that their "connectivity" is a matter for discussion and debate. And it sets the stage for later lectures and discussions of world systems, what they linked, how tight or fragile they were, and what their legacy was. When I taught the course in 2008, I talked about the oft-quoted claim that George Bush was the Genghis Khan of the contemporary age: an effective way to emphasize the use-value of this history for the present. If nothing else, connectivity puts the burden of assessment and interpretation on you and your students, requiring them to take responsibility for the work of *making* connections and defending them, if necessary — requiring them to take responsibility, that is, for the where and the when of the world in world history.

This is not to say that the work of connectivity — as a metaphor, as a positioning device, as an app, or as an engine of critical thinking — is innocent. Nor, as in the lingo of network systems theory in which the term is echoed, is it "unbiased." All design principles have histories and bear the imprints of power. The GPS was developed by the Department of Defense, and if you use it to help students understand what you mean by connectivity, you should produce its histories and its antecedents as well. Nor is this merely a contemporary phenomenon: communication has long been considered "the nerves of government," by empires and would-be empires alike.[19] This kind of "origins" talk is nothing but useful for enabling students to apprehend what's at stake in beginning to imagine the global or the world, in whatever time and place you are teaching it. What's more, there are histories by the millions that can't be captured by connectivity because there have been millions of people across historical time who may not have had durable, if any, links beyond their specific place.[20] The task of accounting for them in world history, and of devising strategies for doing so, remains a huge one that I hope readers will take up, whether they embrace connectivity as a design principle or not. In any case, your classroom is a space of power, of power produced however indirectly by forces of world history. Given that your students are likely to have come of age with more digital savviness than you, connectivity may seem utterly commonsensical to them. This means you have as much to learn from them as they have to learn from world history. Those two pedagogical experiences are,

of course, intimately related, in ways that may upend your whole appre-
hension of the syllabus, the course, and the project of world history itself.
If we prize the dynamic (inter)action of the historical space of the classroom as one ground upon which historical knowledge is produced, let's
hope it does.

Chapter Three

How to Do More than "Include Women"

IN THE DAYS when the study of women and gender was still marginal to the practice of History (capital "H")—which was not so very long ago, historically speaking—the classic response to calls for more attention to one of the world's biggest demographics was that there was simply not enough room on the syllabus or time in the semester to attend to everything else that needed to be covered "plus" women. Unless you are trained as a women's or gender historian (and, frankly, even if you are), grappling with how to organize narratives of world history on whatever scale you choose so that they attend to both the historical experiences of women and the structural forces that have produced gender and sexual difference as matters of life and death, of work and play, of war and peace, of *heimat* and exile, remains hugely challenging. Despite the rich array of sources, both primary and secondary, that are now available to teachers looking for material that integrates women or speaks to the gendered character of big arcs like the worlds that slavery made or units like religious life across, inside, and outside Christendom, how to plot a syllabus that consistently addresses the relationship between women's and gendered histories and the arcs of world history is by no means self-evident.[1] How many times have I heard students with these commitments talk of their undergraduate course experiences, courses in which professors either cordon off women and gender into special sections of lecture on days of the syllabus or, worse, "run out of time" because such topics are what there is room for when there is extra space in a discussion? Even a glance at some of the most popular and well-conceived world history textbooks suggests that women and gender, as categories of evidence and analysis, have not been sufficiently thought through. When they are not treated in passing, as supplements to a prefabricated topic (i.e., when modern democracy is equated with suffrage, and ancient societies with the household), they are often relegated to popular culture or social history, rather than threaded through purposefully and proportionally to clarify their indispensability to comprehensive accounts of the global past. The extent to which women — whether via images, textual fragments, or links to material culture — appear in boxes, set off from the main narrative of textbooks or as a supplement to it, probably warrants some study, if not wholesale consideration by publishing houses interested in total "coverage" in world history.

I have tremendous sympathy for textbook writers on this score, as should we all. Women and gender — by the latter I mean the binary system of differences ascribed to men and women, typically in conjunction with other systems of hierarchy and value like class and race or ethnicity — are just two of many issues that historians who tackle the kind of grand narratives written for world history surveys have to keep in mind as they write and, most likely, as they collaborate with other authors to cover the vast spatial and chronological ground typically required of them. Notwithstanding the volumes of available evidence of women's roles in shaping politics, trade, and culture high and low — whether printed, archival, or in the form of oral testimony — fully historicizing women and gender and related issues is more a matter of what kind of case to make about their significance in world history than about whether to make one at all. But make no mistake: the relative presence or absence of women and gender on your syllabus represents an argument about how you view the world's history and tells the story of world history no less than your choice of how to arrange the chronological and spatial frames of the course. Women and gender matter; they are of material consequence to how students apprehend the worlds you are bringing to their sightline. What are some options for designing your course so that it addresses this question head on?

For some teachers, simply registering women at the sightline of world history is enough — what we used to call the "add women and stir" method. Indeed, it's quite possible to produce a parallel narrative to "great events" by finding and inserting either female or gendered examples that complement those big stories. So you can leaven your lecture on the worlds of the Ottoman empire that tracks "paths to power at the Ottoman court" by juxtaposing those paths with evidence of women of the Mughal empire. Hindu Bhakti poets and the fate of empress Nur Jahan might give a broader geographical context to your examples. Or you can transform your lecture on African responses to colonialism by turning to the memoir of one Baba of Caro, a Muslim Hausa woman who offers an ethnography of both European colonizers and the Fulani royal household.[2] There is ample source material for drilling down into daily life to find ordinary women's experiences, even from all kinds of "texts," as the woodcarvings of the indigenous Peruvian Guaman Poma that show Andean women sowing and doing other forms of labor evocatively illustrate.[3] Having said that, access to women's voices that attest to or represent the full range of historical experience you may want to cover in your course can be limited. You may want to know how a West African slave who experienced the middle passage felt about the journey or about motherhood on a seventeenth-century Caribbean plantation, but you will be hard pressed to find such an account, unless you turn to fiction or rely on the speculations of historians like Jennifer Morgan, who tries her hand at piecing extant fragments together to imagine what such experiences might have looked like.[4] When you are up against the limits of what can be known, you have an invaluable opportunity to help students think about the power of sources both absent and present. Even when you have a slave narrative, say from a later period, and that narrative is the consequence of abolitionist patronage and editorial interventions, you have a chance to think aloud and wrestle with the porous and parlous nature of speech that survives the trauma of world history but is hardly transparent or easy to read, let alone to interpret for its historical meanings and significance.

To be sure, such reckonings can be had in a variety of ways and they are not necessarily dependent on a feminist perspective. Why, you may ask, do we need them? Aren't they just supplemental to the really important stories? As one of the fundamental organizing principles of human societies, gender is "arguably at the base of world history."[5] And, as historians have been arguing for decades, attention to women and gender not only sheds light on the histories of women and the career of gender; it opens other avenues of historical inquiry that would be unavailable by any other means. One of the most obvious examples for American teachers and students is a gendered analysis of a figure like Teddy Roosevelt: soldier, hunter, and influential twentieth-century president. The white, homosocial worlds he circulated in shaped his self-image as a man of action, especially among "savages" and "natives," a phenomenon even a short excerpt from his classic *The Rough Riders* dramatizes.[6] That model of manly heroism shaped America's self-image as the world's policeman and the presidency as a "bully" pulpit in ways that continue to resonate today, with real consequences for local and global understandings of American power, military and otherwise. Admittedly, one of the dangers of specifying women and gender as a major conceptual device in your syllabus is that it can end up as a kind of drop-in, valuable for what it says about power and the past but not, potentially, linked to the connectivity (however you imagine it) that is the motor of your argument about global pasts. Here the Roosevelt example works well because the Rough Rider episode can easily help to give shape to units on U.S. imperialism at the turn of the twentieth century. And because of Roosevelt's affinity for both the British empire and Kipling, his example can also be used to link events like the Boer War and the Spanish American War — each pivotal in their respective imperial contexts but linked forward to the Russo-Japanese conflict and to the coming reconfigurations of the international order at Versailles. In this matrix, gender (which here signifies aspirational white, aristocratic masculinity and the accompanying presumption that women are limited to the domestic sphere) acts not simply as a dimension of identity but as a historical force, knitting all kinds of disparate places and events together in a kinetic, if not exactly seamless, fabric — and allowing students to make connections across empires and centuries that they might not otherwise have been equipped to make. At the very least, gender offers an angle of vision, an access point for apprehending any number of related systems, events, scales, perspectives, and lives.

Given the plethora of male figures as makers of history, the kind of gendered analysis I strive to do with respect to Roosevelt is eminently portable. Adele Perry has done it effectively for one of the first governors of British Columbia and you can imagine the possibilities, no doubt, for countless other famous men.[7] Needless to say, such an analysis works for women as well; when I have occasion to talk about Elizabeth I of England, for example, I open with the argument that contemporaries viewed her as a queen "with the heart and stomach of a king."[8] Given her international dynastic intrigues and the fact that contemporary rulers in Europe were mainly men, that provocatively gendering quote can spin a transnational story about royal power and its fate in the sixteenth century — and the critical role played by women in dynastic power, its continuities and ruptures, as well.[9] A planned, purposeful focus on women, gender, or both, as vehicles for recovering lives or dramatizing processes in several scales, can advance the case you want to make about what a world history looks like and yield a number of benefits beyond attention to women and gender per se. Like a variety of global phenomena that predate modern forms of globalization, the evidence of women's worldliness, let alone their power, in a variety of times and places unsettles students' certainties in the best sense, defamiliarizing the present and adding to your accumulating case about the urgency of knowing the complexities of the past in order to better appreciate claims made about dress, custom, belief, war, childbearing, and the West itself — claims made in and about the present.

How, you may ask, can attention to women and gender advance our appreciation for the work of global forces or processes? How have women, how has gender, acted in global ways? When I teach the early twentieth-century world, I ask students, What difference does it make to us to know that the ideas about gendered revolutionary social order that emanated from the Yucatán during the Mexican Revolution sparked unwarranted concerns on the part of American observers that the new Yucatán governors harbored ties with Bolsheviks and other communists worldwide?[10] And that those same revolutionaries turned to the Mayan woman as the ideal upon which to build a new revolutionary consciousness? Comparisons with Irish nationalism and its return to its so-called feminine Gaelic roots, or comparisons to Indian nationalists' invocation of *Bande Mataram* ("I do homage to the mother") as a kind of national anthem that had the same resonance across roughly the same period, make for important points of connectivity between women and gender and political and social change. In each of these cases, there are individual stories and historical genealogies to be explored in order to give flesh and bone to these epic events. Indeed, you could start with Mexico and end up in Moscow by way of Bengal — or the reverse — in a unit organized around early twentieth-century social upheaval through this connective tissue of women, gender, and revolution, a unit producing unforeseen connections between feminism and regime change across multiple sites and polities. This is the very kind of global argument that a tight and carefully designed focus on women can elucidate, an argument to be aligned with even more sweeping claims about the new global order in the years between 1900 and 1920.

In the transnational scenario I've described above, the woman question — in its connection to actual women and as a vision of new gendered political orders — serves as a kind of illuminating dye, a means of tracking connections across what look at first glance like disconnected movements, but which turn out to be pivoting on similar if not identical structural assumptions and ideological systems, as well as on patriarchal political economies. But more than that, my example shows exactly how portable gendered ideas about nationalism and belonging were and how they shaped the terms and conditions through which revolution itself was conceived and acted on. It shows, in other words, that women and gender were not just carriers of global processes but makers of global histories, both in their own right and in conjunction—and sometimes colli-sion—with a variety of ideas, events, and other historical actors. For as I indicated in chapter 2, connectivity need not mean conductivity, and gender can be seen to work as a break in connection or comparison, espe-cially when it is splintered by class or race. So, for example, as Jean Allman and Victoria Tashjian have shown, Asante women hardly swallowed Euro-pean missionary pronouncements about child rearing or hygiene simply because they were articulated by fellow women; and the history of white, Western, female reform movements is full of similar rejections of or indif-ference to ideas and practices cast as "woman to woman advice."[11] To what degree did some communities of women remain outside global forces, impervious or indifferent to them? My point here is not that women are always superconnective forces or that gender systems necessarily guaran-teed links between women or communities, but rather that examining women and gender as constitutive of historical events, their intercon-nectivity and their catalytic effects, *is a method* for seeing with particular vividness the multidimensionality of world histories.

If we concede that women and gender can make hypervisible the cir-culation of structures of power and their individual agents, as well as the breakdown of such structures and agents, sexuality is an equally powerful conceptual device, mapping as it does the circuitry of power, its capillaries and its consequences for happenings larger than the act of sex itself. Stu-dents need to have a world history vantage point on sexuality because of the ways it has been produced and pathologized by the interests of global capital for several centuries. Presumptions about sexuality—the need to regulate it, normativize it, and codify it—have helped to organize the way people work and worship differently and recognizably across ethnic, racial, and class boundaries and within them as well. Meanwhile, prescrip-tions concerning sexual behavior have done nothing less than shape the very imaginary of modernity for its advocates and critics alike. Considered a potent and dangerous and elemental force of nature in so many differ-ent times and places, sexuality looks so familiar, so apparently universal. Students may scarcely recognize it as having a history, let alone a glob-ally differential one, so that it can, paradoxically perhaps, work amazingly well as a means of clarifying what historical contingency is, how sexuality works through the unfolding of power, and as a sign of that unfolding as well. As with women and gender, histories of sexuality can be used to supplement dominant narratives of power and domination (or conflict and rebellion) that appear to be devoid of all sexual meaning. It's incredible but often true: students who think they know about the Second World War are often stunned to learn about either the rape of German women by Russians on the eastern front or the fact that "comfort women" undergird so much of the logic of the Japanese military complex leading up to and beyond Pearl Harbor.[12] Beyond sexuality as an instrument of global war there is sexuality as a technology of global labor regimes. From the Lowell mills to the diamond mines of South Africa, ideas about sexuality — as the basis for the division of labor or as the specter of miscegenation — are instrumental to the histories of work and profit the world over. Arguments about the constitutive role of sexuality work well, if not best, when sexuality can be seen to work in domains where its impact is unexpected: in spaces where sex and gender appear to be unmarked but can be shown to have tremendous effect. While you might gravitate toward prostitution as emblematic of a history of the global body, planning a lecture or a mini-lesson on the rise of the department store as both a safe and an unsafe space for the modern middle-class woman, from Cairo to Constantinople, might be a more effective way to install sexuality at the heart of a narrative about the gendered, urban modern. Given the associations of the shop counter as a site of trade and exchange, the leap to prostitution is not hard to make, but it places the woman of leisure and the streetwalker in close proximity, thereby dramatizing very specific class histories of sexual respectability and the hierarchies of women's work upon which they depended. Nor are these by any means purely "national" stories, as the history of Australian Chinese money in the making of interwar Shanghai department stores so dramatically underscores.[13]

I am not suggesting, of course, that women and gender are distinct from sexuality — or, for that matter, that sexuality as a field of power is any easier to see than, say, gender.[14] In an introductory world history course, each term acts as a heuristic device, allowing you to accomplish different and interrelated objectives and, ultimately, to demonstrate how histories of gender and sex are intertwined with those of "globalization" at any given moment. As students of history know only too well, what counts as "sexual" or even as a "proper" gender norm is not a given in all times and places. Both depend on which women and men — or girls and boys — are at issue and what kind of gendered bodies are at stake or at play. Early on in my world history course, I use the example of Tlaltelolcan women exposing their genitals to their Aztec enemies in an attempt to resist them. I do so matter-of-factly and in the context of a larger lecture in which I discuss indigenous cosmologies before, during, and after the time of Spanish conquest.[15] But I don't miss the opportunity to ask students to dwell on this image so I can bring home what becomes a distinctive refrain in the course: gender systems are not timeless any more than gender performances are universal, and their specificities tell us as much if not more about historical stasis and change as any other instruments of measurement we might have. One way of teaching "the Columbian encounter," in fact, is as a collision of gender, and gendered, systems.[16] Encouraging students to appreciate how and why this is so cannot be a matter of accident in a syllabus. Women, gender, and sexuality have to be thoughtfully — and, it must be said, routinely — embedded so that they do not appear epiphenomenal or, worse, random, faddish, or sensational. For my part, I announce the centrality of the questions raised by all three concepts at the start of my course; they constitute one of the major conceptual arenas I name on the syllabus itself as part of the rationale for the course, and I am candid about that fact from day one, as I am about where I begin the class and why, and what my views on the global are and why I hold them.

Although I do reference women, gender, and sexuality regularly, at the start of the semester and throughout, I also use the body as a kind of conceptual catch-all, arguing for its capacity to get at the issues that matter for questions of global historical change and power. I suggest where the global has the potential for connectivity in multiple dimensions and via multiple systems of meaning and material reality. For if you are talking about slavery, you must talk about the laboring body, both productive and reproductive, at all stages of the life cycle, and as it pertains to mas-

45

culinity and femininity in tandem. If you are talking about Ming imperialism or Versailles, you have to think about the body of the royal person and its centrality to the creation and maintenance of political and cultural power. If you are describing the Inquisition, whether in Europe or the New World, you cannot but address the body as a site of torture. If you are talking about anticolonial nationalism, you must surely address Gandhi's bodily practices and their centrality to satyagraha, Nelson Mandela's conjugal life and its impact on his antiapartheid activities, and the role of Irish hunger strikes in the iconography of the free state or the republic. For some historians, the whole project of colonial power in its global aspiration rests on the quest to "capture the individual body" through regimes of discipline, surveillance, and occupation.[17] These are more than mere metaphors. Indeed, even Martin Luther's stout build, his physical "monumentality," had a huge impact on Reformation propaganda worldwide.[18] Embodiment itself is a profoundly historical condition, a force to be reckoned with, and one that students can—with the help of historical example—come to appreciate as necessary for a critical understanding of what the global is.

Drawing on Kathleen Canning's claim about the body as a method, as well as on work I have done with Tony Ballantyne on colonial bodies, world history, and bodies as moving subjects (both mobile and affective), I plot my syllabus so that it takes regular account of the body as a historical agent both within and across the times and places I've selected as the basis for my account of world histories.[19] As I've said above, this means turning to the body as an object of inquiry in as many lectures and readings as I can. Sometimes that entails beginning with the body—that of the slave, in my unit on maritime empires and global systems of slavery—and sometimes it means using it to strengthen an argument about comparison or connectivity, as when I talk about absolutism under Suleiman and Louis XIV. And sometimes it means using a concept like motherhood or domesticity to get at the detailed histories of encounter; there the focus is specifically on "bodies in contact" and processes of encountering, mixing, and settling in several historical coincident settings. One advantage of a focus on bodies is that it can allow you to take up a variety of questions related to women, gender, and sexuality when you may not be able to draw on evidence of women, gender, or sexuality per se. You may want to talk about Native American and Métis women in the American midwest in order to get at the gendered character of dynastic relations in and around fur trading, but you may lack the requisite documents that communicate women's voices; or those documents may not exist. But you can read all kinds of historical evidence in traders' books, genealogical accounts, and even maps of the region and period to enable students to imagine how indigenous women's bodies were used and abused in the service of community-building and profit-taking. I juxtapose these stories of economic agency with that of Eva, née Krotoa, a Khoena woman who acted as a translator to the Dutch in their early dealings with Africans on the frontiers of the Cape Colony.[20] Through this kind of "connective comparison" we are able to get at the similarities and differences of encounter, to center women and their embodied experiences in histories of trade and colonization, and to engage the problems of archive and the "recovery" of women's voices.[21] We are also able to pry gender and sexuality loose from their association with identities and see them as agents of power. If the world is a social concept, so too is gender. Getting students to see both as objects of inquiry in their own right, as produced in whatever forms by history itself, is an ongoing challenge of the course.

I want to underscore here, as I do in the life of the class itself, that by attending to women or sexuality in preconquest Mexico or the Cape Colony we are at once building on work we've done around similar issues and anticipating units that are to come—not just about the body per se but about how, through certain kinds of historical forces and evidentiary traces, we can actually assess women's work in global processes, and the work as well of local women in the shape of those processes. Doing more than simply including women depends on creative *and recurrent* methods; above all, it requires a commitment to using those methods and their conceptual cognates as a deliberate and meaningful strategy for building whatever case for world history you are trying to make. Like connectivity and the chronology of the global you have chosen as design principles, the body can give your syllabus an architecture, a frame around which to build your arguments. Or it can be the driver; it can serve both functions at different moments, where necessary or appropriate.

For what it's worth, I am still not satisfied with my own rendition of these questions. And until textbooks take the lead in modeling how to center women and the body in narratives large and small, those who rely extensively on those textbooks will have to find other means for learning not just the histories connected to women and the body but strategies for locating them foundationally in syllabi. Until then, the only way for these questions to make their way to the heart of your syllabus, and of students' experience of world history, is for you to put them there and then to work with them, to assess their success and their limits as you go. Needless to say, students will have strong opinions about these topics: there's nothing like subject matter that smacks of "sex" and "history" to push buttons and stimulate debate. Happily we can all capitalize on that kind of energy to move the conversation about what world history is and should be forward.

Chapter Four

World History from Below

WORLD HISTORY IS OFTEN big history, which is part of what makes it intimidating to newcomers, both teachers and students alike—especially when "big" entails a focus on large-scale processes and systems that span vast arcs of time. Of course, "Big History" (capital "B") is a well-established methodological approach in world history and beyond, one that emphasizes chronologies from the very beginning of time and seeks to juxtapose human history with structural forces and processes that may involve the cosmos and the environment as much as human subjects per se.[1] More colloquially, when "big" means "global" in a syllabus, it can mean that giant phenomena, the kind most often mapped in textbooks, get the most attention, in part because of the pressure for coverage of a common core of topics, or even themes. If you are teaching a world history class to prepare high school juniors or seniors for an AP examination, you may feel the need for huge scope and scale, and for generalizations that can support them in response to the preset expectations of the test. If you are teaching an introductory world history survey that serves as a student's only history course, or her only global humanities course, you too may feel compelled to reach for the most recognizable structures (trade, empire, migration, and war) or signature events (new world conquest, the "scramble" for Africa, or world wars) to give your course shape and to move your chronological narrative, however you frame it, along at the necessary clip. These are certainly reasonable responses to constrained choices. But if you want, in turn, to put some pressure on the global as a category of scale, to get to ground in order to put flesh and bone on big stories, what are some options for locating that maneuver consistently or even occasionally in the architecture of your syllabus? And if you want a history from below to be a major, structural dimension of the course as a whole, what possibilities are there for challenging the top-down narratives of world history and, in the process, equipping students with a working definition of what the global means in discrete historical circumstances? Here it may be useful to make a distinction between the global as an attribute of some kinds of historical events or processes — the "global traffic in women," for example — and the global as a positioning device dependent on where you are looking *from*, as when a North American prairie looks "local" or small but is in fact linked to all kinds of regional and global systems.

One response to the presumption that world history entails a macro view — in academic histories, in public policy, and in NGO activity — has been to counter the juggernaut of the global with assertions of local specificity and particularity. Regrounding the global in the local, you often hear, puts a brake on homogenizing generalizations and at least potentially gives a certain kind of agency to nonstate actors and marginal peoples, making them subjects rather than objects of our world history gaze. There are many advantages to this kind of reorientation. For one thing, you can use local histories as a litmus test for big claims about the impact or even the reach of global processes. If the eighteenth-century "age of revolutions" — taking place in America, Haiti, France, and Latin America — really did have global effects, what influence did the ideas and actions of Thomas Paine, Toussaint L'Ouverture, Olympe de Gouges, and Simón Bolívar have on later movements for democracy? When their ideas or accounts of their actions traveled, how and where did they travel? Did they move only inside a certain geographical sphere, and if so, does that make theirs a global age of revolutions? An age of global revolutions? These are not mere semantic differences. If the former is the answer, your axis of analysis is chronological; if the latter, it's arguably more spatial; and precision on the use of those terms can generate useful lecture material, discussion, or both. Did the work of these rebel leaders trickle down to ordinary people, or make its way into systems of, say, law, that then had an impact on populations, or even elites, below the most privileged? Bourbon reformers in colonial Peru drew on Enlightenment ideas to reshape the legal system and to dictate who counted as a legal subject and who did not. Yet ideas about rights, citizenship, and the limits of "minority" that derived from the global transformations of the revolutionary age (broadly 1650–1820) also opened up avenues in the courts for petitioners to stake their claims to property, child custody, and other kinds of social and political capital. As the research of Bianca Premo has shown, women were "key actors in these suits" in ways that allowed them to make use of legal discourses mediated by a "larger" world of shifting language and possibility to seek local power in the household or extended-family setting.[2] When women came from the countryside to Lima to press these claims, the royal court hardly seemed local to them, of course. Acknowledging these histories requires attention to scale and perspective that potentially reimagines where, as well as how, revolutions in an age of revolutions most meaningfully played out.

If you decide to treat the local as a counter to the big picture, there are as many occasions for drilling down to a microlevel as there are macronarratives. These interventions can be more or less elaborate, and take more or less time away from "the main event" of a class session, depending on your preference, your level of knowledge about a given subject, and the availability of sources that can help you frame your narrative, dig deep, or share with your students via a handout or PowerPoint. If you are doing a lecture on Mao, you might feel that you want to get "below" the conventional narrative of his rise to power but that you don't know enough to stray too far. In that case, careful attention to just one of his essays, "Report on the

Peasant Movement in Hunan," from 1927, might be a start. Presumably you have set up the broad significance of Mao's "continuous revolutions," their spatial reach and their impact outside China proper. This might be a moment, by turning to peasant and rural uprising, to get specific about Mao's determination to root the struggle not at the national or even the provincial level but "in local society." The pamphlet from 1927 is ideal for this because it makes the case that such insurrections fulfilled the promise of Sun Yat Sen's 1911 Revolution and because it also makes a stark contrast with China's revolution and "the urban revolution[s] promised by European Marxism." You have a chance to situate the report and Mao's philosophy of communist revolution in a time scale with both Chinese and European referents, and to enable students to appreciate just exactly what Mao meant when he said, "Revolution is not a dinner party."[3]

Another option is to start with a ground-level example and build up from there, to offer students a glimpse of how global processes look from the point of view of those who experience them, those who might therefore be considered global subjects. Did they experience themselves as such subjects? And if not, is it right for us to label them as such? An example I am very familiar with and use often is the tea drinker in nineteenth-century Britain. Her beverage of choice — which is to say, the beverage of her status, if she were middle class — came to her via any number of far-flung imperial and semiimperial possessions, especially if we count the sugar in the bottom of the tea cup, which likely came from Caribbean plantations. If she lived before the 1830s she might have been aware of these origins because the abolition movement in Britain stemmed from the late eighteenth century. If she grew up in the shadow of 1833, the year of the Slavery Abolition Act, and if she were a Quaker or a print culture reader, she may well have been aware of the storm of popular protest and political activity that surrounded the act. She might even have been drawn into the sugar boycotts that abolitionists organized, and she might, as many British feminists did, have acquired some associational and organizing experience that drew her or her daughter into the women's suffrage movements of the late 1850s and early 1860s, of which John Stuart Mill and his wife Harriet Taylor were the leading lights.[4] Here the local is Britain, and your focus on the female tea drinker opens out onto a host of issues, not least the tense and tender ties between white English women and the Caribbean slaves they patronized, in word, image, and deed, to give moral luster and bathos to their cause. Such women had lives and agendas of their own. Mary Prince, a former slave from Bermuda, wrote her own personal, political history, which works well as a counternarrative to the stories big and small that emerge from the tea table.[5] When students know that Chinese and Turkish women of rank also drank tea at table, they come to understand how the consumer revolution linked modern bourgeois imaginaries, at least in global terms. Indeed, these so-called local stories reveal the entanglement of the tea table in wider webs of empire, trade, and commerce, raising the question: Which of these players saw themselves operating in a global context? And is an imperial context ever a global context? Are the two overlapping after 1850 but not before?

When I use the local as a teaching tool I generally do so in two ways: to give what anthropologists call "thickness" to an ostensibly big process and to cut that process down to size so that students can better appreciate what a perspectival term "global" actually is. Our tea-drinking abolitionist may well have viewed herself as a global consumer, aided in that identity by the pressure of historical events in her lifetime or by an awareness of them as part of her birthright as an imperial Briton. Did the Welsh working man who drank tea for a different reason — for the energy its caffeine and sugar gave him for a ten- to fifteen-hour day in the mines — see his drink as leverage on the same kind of global identity? Did either of them imagine the tea-picker in Assam, or were their sights set on the Caribbean plantation, rather than the Asian plantation, as the site of political pedagogy?[6] And does that mean that their sense of worldliness was actually more limited than they or their contemporaries realized? Because one of the most important projects of world history in the last two decades has been to break from a presumptively Eurocentric model, one that posits a kind of fortress Europe at the center of narratives of history, using the local as a tool for calling out residual traces of that from-West-to-the-rest narrative can work very well. Starting with the "coolie" labor — whether Chinese or Indian — that picked tea, slashed cane, and helped deliver increasingly popular commodities like sugar and caffeinated beverages to westerners of all ranks pivots this whole account on a different axis, of course, and enables you to see the work of "the below" in framing global processes, rather than simply reacting to them.

As a British historian, one of my favorite examples of the kind of spatial reorientation that thinking about above and below can accomplish comes from Rebecca Karl's work on the rise of Chinese nationalism and internationalism at the beginning of the twentieth century. Her research shows how the Chinese globalized one of the most important moments in modern "British" history, the Boer War (1899–1902), *at the very time of its happening.* Karl demonstrates that the war was just one of several critical eruptions at this pivotal moment in world history, alongside the Spanish American War, the decline of the Ottoman empire, and the annexation of Hawaii. Historians of the Anglo-American empires commonly join these events in their own narratives, but Karl shows how Chinese observers anticipated this maneuver and cast events in South Africa and in the circum-Pacific from their end of the telescope, magnifying them in terms of developments in Hawaii and the Philippines in order to serve their own growing imperial, transnational ambition. In Karl's account, the fin-de-siècle conflict in South Africa was not a singular, pivotal moment that defined Britain's global power but was, rather, one of several events that looked decidedly local from the vantage point of Beijing.[7] Of course, Karl is dealing mainly with elite sources. But what I like about this example is that you can pivot it in your syllabus from any number of geographical points on the map with the goal of asking students to consider where exactly the local is local, when and for whom it is local. And you can challenge the centrality of the British empire, its status at and as the pinnacle of global power as well. What the Chinese scholar Liang Qichao (1873–1929) said of the First World War might just as easily be applied to the transnational, multiimperial Boer War: the war "is not a manuscript for a new world history, but it is a transition that continues many elements from above and opens up new ones for the space below."[8]

And yet I have to say that although I do use the local as a repositioning device in this way, and it can be effective, it also makes me uneasy. For when the local is only ever that which "grounds" the global, we are not really breaking up the top-down narrative or necessarily querying the scale of the global. We are just acknowledging the supremacy of the big stuff and filling out the details of the small stuff. And our model of connectivity is decidedly vertical, rather than horizontal, cutting in one direction rather than crosshatching or slicing through a variety of spaces and times. What's more, "below" invariably seems lesser: less big, less significant, less powerful, less representative, less important (especially on the test; for more on that, see chapter 10, "Testing (for) the Global). It seems to me that there are two disadvantages to this when teaching world history. If the local is typically "down there" — or in east-west terms, "over there" — it's harder to mount a critique of a Euro-American-centered narrative, in which the local will always look simply like a version of the global or, worse, its pale imitator. So indigenous forms of rule end up looking either primitive, undemocratic, or derivative of Western norms. The same obtains for cosmologies and arts of healing; for poetry and science; and for gender norms and expectations. As Jean Allman and I have written elsewhere, the historian must resist the persistent fiction that the indigenous is always local and that the local is "merely waiting to be superseded by the transnational or the global, rather than acting as a galvanizing (if not the galvanizing) force in the continual making and remaking of those domains in all their apparent 'historical newness.'"[9] And if the local is always posited below the global, at a metaphorical ground level, the temptation is to think vertically, in a grid where all the power and culture resides or emanates from the top and simply trickles down to passive masses who respond but never initiate — and hence leave little mark on "real" history, world history or otherwise.[10] In these scenarios, if you only treat the local as a kind of lowercase example of a big-ticket subject, you not only miss a huge and substantial slice of history's happenings, your sense of interconnectivity is unidirectional, rather than multidirectional. To be sure, sometimes those vectors *are* north-south and top-down; there's no more sense in denying that power has historically worked that way than there is in denying that everything from political institutions to religious organizations to social movements to gender systems have been organized hierarchically, with those on top (and some in the middle) profiting and those on the bottom suffering or losing out. But if we know anything as historians, we know this kind of transhistorical generalization is insupportable; Generalizations are not, perforce, always the case and, as importantly, they are not everywhere the case. If we only plot a global-local grid that operates vertically, we end up with a much less reliable picture of global pasts than we have the capacity to craft.

How to get around this problem? Teachers of world history are certainly not the first to ask whether we can acknowledge that "places are not so much singular points as constellations, the product of all sorts of social relations which cut across particular locations in a multiplicity of ways."[11] How to do just this remains an animating concern, a real irritant, for the field and for historians more generally. I doubt you will find one textbook that solves the problem of thinking "from below" across all examples, all themes, and all chapters. But you can keep it alive in your syllabus in a variety of ways. The most obvious solution is to start with the structural below, ideally with a primary source. I can suggest Tran Bu Bunh's *Red Earth*, a memoir of a rubber-plantation worker in French Indochina, as an effective text for trying to reverse the hierarchy of top-down views of global production and consumption and to expose students not just to "the hell on earth" of such a life and such a world, but to the ways rubber workers shape the global flow of goods and the world economic system.[12] You can also seek and use examples that cut a horizontal path across time and space, even if they also partake in real and powerful hierarchies of power. Indentured migration is an excellent example, in part because of its virtually global character in the modern period. An outcropping of a variety of slave systems, indenture entailed the forced movement of vast numbers of people, mainly people of color, either from one location to another (China to the United States, let's say) or from one location to several (people of South Asian descent from all over the Indian Ocean world to the Caribbean, Mesopotamia, Malaysia, and beyond). Of course, indentured laborers were subject to power: they were mainly taken against their will, committed to servitude, and subject to the lash and worse. And though they were scattered across the globe, they were seen as the legal and geopolitical responsibility of sovereign nations and empires. And yet despite the fact that these laborers were enmeshed in vertical hierarchies, mainly juridical, that positioned them as decidedly below, they were seconded all over the map and their presence remade the communities in which they found themselves with consequences for world history. The Indian diaspora in South Africa that helped to make Gandhi who he became in the twentieth century is just the most famous example; there are myriad others less central even to what are considered the "main" events and players of world history. The circulation of Chinese labor in Australasia was instrumental not just to the process of nationhood in the antipodes but to the militant whiteness of their foundational legal, educational, and population policies.[13] When you pay attention to the demographics of indentured labor and settlement in global terms, you have to rethink conventional, spatial maps in ways that are especially useful for American students. When we see how and why West Indian coolies were transplanted to a nineteenth-century segregated U.S. South, we get a whole new appreciation of globalization in the "age of emancipation."[14] When we hear that Japanese immigrants refer to California as a "Japanese slope," the racial complexity of America's claim to being the global melting pot is made visible, and we gain some sense of how people "at the bottom" reconfigured hegemonic geographies that many of us take for granted.[15]

A focus on pilgrimage can function as another such lateral thread, and offers one way to map big demographics and small stories — whether via the memories of Hajj travelers or Chaucer — that link disparate parts of the world and can animate early modern or modern timeframes. Again, you can start these stories wherever they make sense to you, place-wise — in Europe, Central Asia, or Saudi Arabia — and you can compare and contrast them with other histories of mass mobility past and present. The sailor, the pirate, and the smuggler are also good for tracking history "under the radar," for revealing political economies that shaped their ages, and for offering a view from the bottom of the social pyramid that can help students rethink dominant narratives and notions of authority and revolution in several places at once.[16] You can and should work to show

how deep the impression of vertical power was on such underdogs. But you can also profitably use them to cross cut that grid and to map a contrapuntal geography of world history. Finding agency and resistance there can be challenging, given the nature of archives, the question of literacy, and the relationship of top-down power structures to what remains, even in terms of oral history and unwritten memory. Verene Shepherd's *Maharani's Misery* — a book that uses primary documents from the court case of a laborer who was killed and probably raped on a ship carrying her from Calcutta to Guyana to reconstruct the conditions of indenture — is one of a number of available sources that can help you do this work.[17] As students of the slave trade and of other oceanic histories know, the ship itself is an extraordinarily useful teaching tool: it is produced and controlled by the interests of capital or protocapital and, yet, between ports, it is sometimes possible to glimpse the interruption of distinctions between upper and lower decks, between the bird's-eye view afforded by the captain's perch and the deep below of the galleys. Though slave and sailor voices are notoriously hard to hear, they do exist, and they can be reconstructed from a variety of sources — especially when historians are creative and students, in turn, are encouraged to listen carefully.[18] Attention to the kinds of moving spaces ordinary people of all kinds inhabited, and to the movement of ideas, goods, and bodies in dynamic tension with those spaces, keeps the horizontal and the vertical always in play. If you succeed in demonstrating even a few instances of where the interdependence between people and the spaces they inhabit is in evidence, you have conjured, perhaps, a metaphor for history in global motion: power at work when it travels between places, whether north-south, east-west, or in vectors that cross and exceed both axes.

Thinking world history from below, as I have tried to begin to do here, is one way of responding to exhortations from many quarters to reterritorialize the globe in contradistinction to civilizational paradigms that students of the field have been involved in defusing, if not always decentering, over the last two decades. Despite the complexities of such paradigms, they tend to be single or unified center models that create an "us" and "them" binary that may obtain in some specific historical times and places but in the main fails to capture the richness and complexity of how kingdoms, nations, commonweals, estates, and even empires operate in practice. Producing a world history syllabus that is open to a variety of territorial configurations that are shifting in response to the dynamism of history large and small may help you and your students break out of the hierarchy of "up top" versus "down below." One effective way to do this, of course, is to create a syllabus that operates wholly from the point of view of the so-called global south: the world from Africa, Latin America, and the Pacific. Iris Berger's *South Africa in World History* and Warren Cohen's *East Asia at the Center* are two places for the nonspecialist to begin.[19] In these cases your "bigs" will be particular to those vantage points, your "belows" will reverse differently (though you could certainly engage with questions of class and resistance), and your trails of connectivity may lead laterally, though they will certainly move vertically as well. Depending on your training, you might find this very challenging, even too challenging, to do across an entire syllabus. If that's the case, what you *can* do is to talk openly and honestly with your students about why this is so hard, and focus at strategic moments on examples that throw into bold relief the geography of east-west or north-south you may be working with. Those are the teaching moments that can have the biggest payoff, but they have to be purposefully placed and thought through as part of a larger syllabus narrative. Needless to say, this is equally true if you organize your whole syllabus around lateral connections, circulations and flows, ocean basins or technoscapes. Just as the bird's-eye view is never the view from nowhere, so too each model you mobilize has to be grounded in historical specificity and will rarely, if ever, be portable across all times and spaces. This is not defeat, nor should it induce paralysis. It's simply one of the occupational hazards of teaching world history.

PART II

Devising Strategies

IN THIS SECTION OF THE PRIMER, I offer specific examples of how to operationalize global narratives and develop models of global interaction, disintegration, or both in your lectures and discussions. Although there are many ways to go about this, I focus on events, genealogies, and empire as teaching tools. And while the examples I offer can be used independently of these particular teaching tools, the strategies in this section reference the foundational principles laid out in PART I. The following strategies proceed, in other words, from the assumption that they are a means for realizing the pedagogical commitments in PART I.

──── *Chapter Five* ────

The Event as a Teaching Tool

ONE OF THE GREATEST pedagogical challenges of world history is finding ways to encourage students to think globally. That probably sounds redundant, and in many ways it is. Aren't histories of the world by definition global? Don't they automatically provide a narrative of interconnection across time and space? Yes and no. Anyone who has faced a world history syllabus assignment for the first time knows how tempting it is to construct a narrative of "the world" that piles up location after location in order to fulfill the multisited promise of the course. This cafeteria approach is not necessarily fatal, and for those who have limited resources it may be the only option they have. But we still need to ask how we can develop skills in our students that are methodological as well as additive, integrative as well as inclusive — especially since additions and inclusions presume a stable center to which "others" can be assimilated, rather than create a toolkit for understanding when the global comes into play, how it manifests itself, and, of course, what evidence we use for determining its histories. World history, at its best, is not simply inclusive of a variety of times and places. At its most ambitious, it cultivates ways of thinking that are expressly but complexly spatial; ways of thinking that map historical phenomena in at least two dimensions (time and space) and that question the possibilities and limits of a "global" view itself.

How do we operationalize these ambitions in concrete pedagogical terms? One effective method for encouraging this kind of skill set is to focus on events with reverberations beyond their points of origin, events with tendrils into and tributaries from a set of global contexts — contexts that not only complicate the traditional understanding of what might be a well-known story but have the capacity to resituate it in a multidimensional context. It's probably easiest to do this with a dramatic and well-known event, one that has a reputation for a kind of one-dimensional spatial story but which you reinterpret to underscore a multidimensional context. I teach Columbus's "discovery" of the New World with these ambitions in mind. I begin with the children's poem, "In Fourteen Hundred and Ninety-Two, Columbus Sailed the Ocean Blue," and then I read aloud from the Wikipedia version of the Columbian exchange narrative. I do this on the assumption that if you want to demonstrate the difference a global interpretation makes, you have to model what a "nonglobal" account looks like. You have to acknowledge the familiar and then denaturalize it. I am then quite open about how I hope to nuance their basic understanding of this "event" by reorienting their gaze through a variety of pivots. My lecture outline (which students have ahead of time and is also projected behind me in the classroom) promises to (1) resituate that narrative in world history by underscoring the global ambition of Spain, its determination to create and secure a species of ecclesiastical imperialism; (2) to draw attention to the competing cosmologies, the collision of spiritual and cultural worlds, that ensued; and (3) to address how this conquest, like all imperial projects, required the remaking not just of the spiritual, economic, and political order, but the gender order as well.[1]

Anyone with even superficial knowledge of the age of Columbus can see, I think, that this is not rocket science. To accomplish the first goal — resituating Columbus in a wide geographical ambit — I link the history of the Reconquista (also 1492) with the moment of discovery, enabling students to appreciate the simultaneity of conquests in Europe and beyond the Atlantic — *and* the hybrid religious worlds that characterized medieval Spain.[2] This is part of my attempt to make a case for the ambitions of an imperial Christendom that are transregional, if not global in scope, and attempt to integrate local neighboring territories with more distant ones. The vast spatial reach of the Inquisition — from Europe to New Spain and back again — is helpful in this regard, and a discussion of the spiritual and religious convictions involved in the Inquisition, and their entanglements with political and economic factors, leads nicely into my second goal, a discussion of cosmologies in conflict. For that lecture, students have been assigned Rebecca Overmyer-Velázquez's essay, "Christian Morality in New Spain," and recourse to that material in lecture allows me to link the "worlds" of indigenous belief and practice that collide with Catholic conversion directly to bodies on the ground via Overmyer-Velázquez's discussion of Nahua women and their challenges to the worldview and colonizing intentions of the Franciscan Bernardino de Sahagún.[3] In this context then, the worlds of 1492 are multiple geographically and in terms of scale. Needless to say, and thanks to a variety of imperial and colonial sources, I put the question of scope and scale directly into play by asking students to ask themselves where conquest happens, how fully it happens, and what the possibilities and limits of this New World moment might be said to mean.

Although I don't begin my course with Columbus's discovery, preferring the vibrant, multiaxial worlds of the fourteenth century as my point of departure, it does come fairly early on in the syllabus and, as a result, serves as an example of one kind of global narrative to which we return during the semester as we hold up and measure other histories. I set the discovery up as one "pivotal" example, and I consolidate it as such as we move into other examples. I try to calcify Columbus's discovery in student's minds as a specific kind of global story, but not as the only way that globality manifests or can be interpreted. Because I have built the limits of integration into that story (using native peoples like the Nahua), and because I have routed that interpretive framework through a story about gendered social-sexual order, those elements are also, and equally, touch-stones for evaluating what counts as a global event as we move along. Admittedly, it's very challenging to find events that work so well along these lines; and, of course, the whole syllabus doesn't pivot on such events, nor could it or should it. But there are moments throughout the course when I purposefully refer back to the example of 1492 so that we can see it as one example, and so that students can develop a critical perspective on the spatial, temporal, and evidentiary standards for considering an event as global — or not.

Another readily available example of how to pivot a lesson regarding the global on a well-known event is through a discussion of the Treaty of Versailles of 1919, which many students learn in high school was the event that marked both the end of the First World War and set the stage for an emasculated Germany and the events leading to the Second World War. They also learn, and rightly so, that Woodrow Wilson's role was extremely important both at the conference itself and in terms of his construction of the famous Fourteen Points as a guide for international diplomacy and the League of Nations. Thanks to the work of Erez Manela, whose book *The Wilsonian Moment* is a primer itself in a certain kind of global history approach, I've developed a lecture in which I reorient Versailles spatially, so that its global dimensions are more fully illuminated — and so that its reverberations through the long twentieth century are more fully understood.[4]

To relocate the treaty of Versailles in a world history context is to enable students to see that at the end of the event-filled year of 1919 the world tilted, if not turned, on a different axis than it had before. In nearly every quarter of the developing and developed world, the social and political order was challenged. From Chicago to Shanghai, people from all walks of life and from all parts of the globe were pushing the limits of the possible in order to make the most of the possibilities of postwar realignment. They sought to realize their political, economic, social, and cultural aims. One way of assessing this tectonic shift is to consider the claims that multiple constituencies made on the Versailles treaty proceedings and the role that the failure of Egyptian, Indian, Chinese, and Korean nationalists had in the fate of anticolonial movements and revolutions in those places. Though it is little known in typical textbook accounts of the treaty, activists from regions outside the West drew on the Wilsonian ideal of national self-determination, as it was enshrined in the Fourteen Points, and used it as the basis for arguments about their right to participate in the shaping of the terms of the postwar order, specifically at the moment of its reconfiguration in 1919 but more generally as part of what they viewed as a watershed moment in the history of geopolitics. So, for example, Saad Zaghlul of Egypt and Lala Lajpat Rai of India were actively engaged in campaigns to present their cases for independence directly to Woodrow Wilson. They used established networks to broadcast the opening that they believed Versailles represented and their own convictions about how and why nationalists should harness the liberal ideals being used as the basis for the postwar settlement to advance their own programs for self-government. Although they, along with Wellington Koo of China and Syngman Rhee of Korea, were the public face of this effort, they each represented deeper nationalist constituencies, whose energies and organizational frameworks they drew on to advance their claims for independence. In the process, they articulated varying degrees of admiration for the United States as an exemplar of civilization, liberty, and global leadership.[5]

That Versailles foundered in part because of the failed bid of the Japanese for equality in explicitly racial terms reveals much about the underpinnings of the new internationalism and offers us, as teachers of world history, endless possibilities for tracking Versailles's presumptive globality across several national borders at once. Centering the story on Japan and East Asia more generally enables us to appreciate the very real limits of America's worldly vision for the twentieth century and to see other avenues of connectivity and rupture in geopolitical terms, as well — including the way that a kind of global whiteness was consolidated at a moment of racial challenge on multiple fronts.[6] Wilson, for his part, used the work of non-Western movements to justify his own agenda at Versailles without taking full account of how his particular brand of liberal internationalism might impact colonial people seeking independence from European imperialism. The result was a series of "empty chairs" at Versailles — for despite their protestation, Indian and Egyptian delegates were not seated at the table in Paris—and, in short order, a series of violent disturbances occurred around the world. In the wake of 1919, it must have seemed to contemporaries as if the world were on fire: there were riots, revolutions, and rebellions in India and Egypt, in London and Chicago—to name just a few sites where postwar dissatisfaction and disappointment with Versailles reverberated across a global landscape, reverberations enabled in part by war and its failed aftermath. Although I haven't used it myself, this example seems like a good one for "concept mapping"—a method of visualizing relationships between concepts (in this case, events) that is graphic and nonlinear. In a lecture format, such mapping might plot Versailles at the center but could do the same with May Fourth, thus allowing students to see connections or disconnections between sites and actors. As a note-taking exercise, this kind of mapping enables students to grasp the shared historical space between events that conventional outlines or written notes might not.[7]

The shifts in national power and imperial stability that resulted from the global reverberations of 1919 played out in a variety of ways. African and Indian nationalists felt emboldened by the slight and launched nothing less than a frontal assault on European claims to being civilized and fair-minded. Women who met at the Hague in 1915 and eventually in the Women's International League for Peace and Freedom in 1919 performed the same script, demanding women's suffrage and making other claims to citizenship not just in Europe, but in Egypt, India, and Turkey, and in Iran as well. Indeed, the interwar years witnessed no fewer than three congresses of Eastern women: in Damascus, Tehran, and Baghdad, where large numbers of mainly educated women gathered to demand the right to participate in politics as equal subjects.[8] The question we have to ask in the end, of course, is what the relationship was between what happened at Versailles and the uprisings in various imperial territories across the globe in 1919 and after. Any answer to that question requires a recognition that from the point of view of anticolonialism on the ground, Versailles served as a catalyst rather than a monocausal agent—it provided a rallying point around which critics of empire could test the application of "new" theories of global order to their own protonationalist movements. In the case of India, Rai was part of a much larger constellation of anti-imperial critics, many of whom had affiliations with the Indian National Congress and had been fighting for recognition in the British empire for decades. The events at Amritsar in 1919 — where British troops fired on Punjabis who gathered to celebrate the traditional spring festival of Baisakhi in the wake of several protests against British rule — are not necessarily traceable directly back to Versailles, though the disillusion produced by the failure of self-determination at Paris undoubtedly contributed to the long-term movement toward *purna swaraj* (complete independence). The same may be said for China, where the May Fourth Movement erupted in the wake of bitter disappointment at Versailles but emanated from several decades of reform aimed at transforming the precarious Qing regime. In this sense, Versailles — where the concession of former German colonies to Japan fed larger concerns about the further aggrandizement of Japanese imperial power — was a "trigger," rather than a root cause.[9] Given that in the wider debates occurring in 1919 and its aftermath, racial equality came to be conceptualized in terms of an international right, this particular trigger set all kinds of global histories in motion.[10]

If 1919 was a pivotal moment, then, not all of its eventfulness can be tracked to Versailles and its aftershocks. Needless to say, the Bolshevik revolution of 1917 altered the global imperial landscape in immeasurable ways, not least because in addition to spawning a Soviet empire whose territorial reach and economic power would rival that of its twentieth-century competitors, it modeled an alternative route to a kind of new world order that the failed experiments in liberal internationalism illuminated for Indian, and especially Chinese, nationalists. The Comintern (also known as the Third International), founded in 1919 and the sponsor of seven congresses in the interwar period, was a key player here. If we view the interwar period from the pivot of the Comintern-sponsored Baku Congress of 1920, where global anticolonial revolution was tabled and delegates attended from India, China, Turkey, Azerbaijan, and Persia, we would glimpse the antiimperialist aspirations of Bolshevism in Asia and beyond.[11] Although the Comintern did not live much beyond the late 1930s, one of its affiliates, the League Against Imperialism, was expressly designed to link anticolonial movements in Afro-Asia and Latin America. Interwar black internationalism, which took off with historically unprecedented velocity in the interwar period, looked as much to Moscow as anywhere else, and grew in part out of a disillusion with Versailles that was predicated on the total exclusion from the mechanisms whence the treaty's mandates had been created, as Marcus Garvey and other "new Negro" intellectuals were determined to point out.[12]

There were also upheavals in and around 1919 — like the foundation of the Irish Republic and the creation of the Anglo-Irish Treaty — whose origins had only a tangential relationship with events at Versailles. As with anticolonial agitation elsewhere, Irish republicanism had a long, variegated history and was shaped by a variety of imperial encounters at all levels that at once preceded and were transformed by the interwar years. The Dáil's "Message to the Free Nations of the World," released during its first meeting in January 1919, claimed, "The race, the language, the customs and traditions of Ireland are radically distinct from the English. Ireland is one of the most ancient nations in Europe, and she has preserved her national integrity, vigorous and intact, through seven centuries of foreign oppression." That claim certainly bears traces of Versailles's rhetoric.[13] To be honest, I struggle with how to keep the embodied histories of this era alive, in part because there are so many ways to do so. The actual treaty table at Versailles is useful, marking out in spatial terms how bodies were arranged and dramatizing who was in and who was out. That women did seek inclusion is clearly key, as is the outbreak of epidemics worldwide as the treaty talks began, an outbreak that not only impacted the body politic from Cairo to Chicago but shaped how welfare systems, with their particular attention to the health of women and children, emerged, or didn't, in the interwar period. For what it's worth, I tell the story of my grandmother and the flu pandemic of 1918. Some in her small northwestern Pennsylvania town died, and she lost all her teeth.

What is clear is that in the wake of Versailles, social and political orders of all kinds — Western, Asian and Eurasian, local, regional, and global — had to adjust to the new ideological and territorial conditions produced

by Wilson's new world order. The formative impact of 1919 on Mao Zedong is probably the best-known example of this: his scornful response to
the "robbers" of Versailles was characteristic of his later leadership, and of
the geopolitical vision he articulated throughout the rest of the twentieth
century, sometimes to a Chinese audience and sometimes to a global one.
Less well known perhaps are the conditions that the interwar years created for figures like Lamine Senghor, the French West African radical, and
the Vietnamese revolutionary Ho Chi Minh, whose work in Paris in the
1920s, in part through the Union Intercoloniale, laid critical foundations
for anti-French colonial movements in Africa and Vietnam.[14]

In the end, the reverberations of Versailles spread unevenly across the
unstably imperial post-1919 world, and gains for imperial powers and resistant actors could be both partial and short-lived. But those gains begin
to indicate some of the ways the interwar period, with its new solidarities
and its capacity for lateral as well as vertical connections, would anticipate the global struggles of the rest of the century. These histories demonstrate why it's important to think spatially, in terms of comparisons and
webs and reverberating events when we think about teaching world history. As I represent it in my course, 1919 offers a different kind of global
pivot than 1492. The similarities and differences between the two make
a useful reference point in the conversation I try to keep in play across
the whole syllabus, a conversation about the contingent forms of worldliness that world history can help us see. Because of my own commitment
to the question of connectivity, I have chosen events whose impact radi-
ates beyond its immediate geographical and temporal specificity, but you
need not be limited to or by that. Indeed, in this chapter I have modeled
out two conventionally "western" or Europe-centered events in order to
prize open that geography and to encourage students to think about what
world histories look like and what a global interpretation can do.

Yet all manner of examples could work in a similar way. Start with the
shovel that inaugurated the first track for the Baghdad-Berlin railway and
follow it through Damascus to Armenian genocide, oil, and beyond.[15]
Take California's Alien Land Law of 1913 and connect it to the women's
antipass law campaign in South Africa and you have the basis for a world

history lecture on the character of agrarian "reform" and resistance.[16] Use the Red Turban revolt of 1351 to create your narrative of the rise and fall of the Ming dynasty. Screen images of the Johnstown flood of 1889 and work backwards or forwards in time and space to take up the question of geophysical patterns and "disasters" either as a one-off unit or as part of a global environmental history syllabus. Begin with someone's birth date — Lorenzo de' Medici, Harriet Tubman, or Ho Chi Minh — and conjure their worlds from there. Choose a nameless peasant or slave with no verifiable birth date and make use of that anonymity to question an event-based approach. I myself have used the death of rapper Tupac Shakur in 1996 to move back in time to Túpac Amaru's rebellion of 1781 in Peru, and then to his ancestor's execution by the Incas in 1572. Sanjay Subrahmanyam spins an early modern world story on 1605, at the deathbed of Akbar.[17] Admittedly, this is just one way of approaching world history, and it won't satisfy all the demands placed on that vast and urgently important project. And, as must be clear, setting one fulcrum in motion, making one "event" visible in a global history course, can be used to show not a singular phenomenon but overlapping processes, what Janet Abu-Lughod calls "multiple cores proliferating."[18] Like other possibilities in this primer, using events as fulcrums — whether as an occasional strategy or a more recurrent design principle — requires planning, especially if links across ostensibly discrete happenings are to drive your narratives. But I think that by emphasizing the spatiality of events and contexts, the lateral connections that may join them, and the nature of some of the evidentiary bases for this pivotal view, we can generate a variety of creative and usable models for how to countenance the teaching of history in ways that capture some of its global possibilities.

Chapter Six

Genealogy as a Teaching Tool

ON OCCASION I HAVE used Billy Joel's song "We Didn't Start the Fire" either as an opener to my world history course or as an entry point into the post-1945 portion of it. The America-centrism of the song, which Joel (b. 1949) wrote to commemorate his fortieth birthday, is a useful point of departure for asking what world has been burning and turning, from what perspective, and why. There are lots of places on the internet where you can download the lyrics and the video. There's so much to be said about this song—from its baby boom denialism, to its male sports orientation, to its juxtaposition of verbal images—which is what makes it such a flexible teaching tool. It models a very specific kind of global perspective, one that students in the United States may identify with, though I suspect the generation for whom it is an immediately recognizable tune is long gone from introductory-level classrooms, at least those populated by students eighteen to twenty years old. One critic has called the song "pure information overload," a catch-phrase that neatly summarizes how many students and teachers feel about the subject of world history.[1] I invoke Billy Joel's song less as a model than as a provocation. For in addition to addressing the global dimensions of the processes and events of world history, should we not also be producing genealogies that make visible the multisited, interconnected, *and* disintegrative pasts of those phenomena or processes that may or may not seem visible at first glance? Attending to the global character of histories that have appeared to be national, regional, local, civilizational, or otherwise bounded is one of the main strategic interventions of world history as a method and a practice. And in keeping with our principled skepticism about the transhistorical nature of the past, it's one way of allowing students to interrogate both the reach and limits of the global as a tool for historicizing—that is, accessing genealogies and histories—a host of contemporary concerns and subjects: environmentalism, poverty, militarism, indigeneity, free trade, Chinese economic growth, evangelism, tourism, the book, movies, insurgency, catastrophe, and, of course, history and globalization as well.

A genealogy is a backstory: the history of how X or Y came to be, was shaped, emerged. The virtue of a genealogical strategy is that virtually any subject can sustain it. The challenge in a world history syllabus is to use a "backstage" approach to cultivate students' appreciation for the past as a tool for honing their convictions about what counts as the global and their ability to assess the legitimacy or persuasiveness of such a claim for any given subject or object. Simply put, everything has a genealogy, a set of origins, and we can't understand anything fully unless we know something about its history. Does everything that is labeled global have a global history? Sometimes. Histories that seem self-evidently bounded—like those of the nation—can have global histories, too. Are there events and processes that operate outside, alongside, and in tension with what we nominate as global? Sometimes. If and when that's the case, we need to help students see exactly how thinking *historically* might forward, nuance, or challenge what students imagine the global and even world history to be. Here we have the chance to bring history alive as a discipline, and as an interdiscipline, whose protocols and procedures serve not simply to register or reveal the global but to act as an evaluative and interpretive force on it. Through genealogical strategies, we have the capacity to model how indispensable history is for global thinking, global studies, global critique, and engaged, informed global citizenship.

Although I endeavor to raise these questions and make these points across the whole of my world history syllabus, there is one subject that lends itself particularly well to the kind of critical work I am advocating here: the traditional "world wars" of the last century (1914–18 and 1939–1945). With worldliness already attached to them, and with students aware more or less of the fact that they happened sometime in the twentieth century (whenever that was!), they make a useful target for a global genealogy lesson. Let me focus here on the First World War. I have a session I called "Rehearsal for the Great War" in which I set up the traditional narrative explanation for the war's outbreak: entente, détente, the Great Powers, Sarajevo, the Black Hand, insurgent nationalisms, and economic crisis — a standard textbook account. I spend a fair amount of time giving depth and detail to this account. I want to consolidate the war for students as a conflict with multiple axes, even "Axis" Powers, and I want students to appreciate what a tentacled history it is, even if we simply maintain a European or Euro-American frame of reference and reach back to the Napoleonic Wars and the Congress of Vienna. As generations of history teachers know, "The Concert of Europe" — the balance of power that eventuated from Vienna and helped to shape European diplomacy and war into the twentieth century — is itself a very useful metaphor for the organized yet complex, and above all dynamic, internationalism that underwrote Western modernity at the site of geopolitics and "world" order. Given the role of Russia on the world stage across this long period, not to mention the shifting boundaries of Europe proper at almost every turn, the symbolic and material impact of the Ottomans on "European" history down to 1918 and the angular relationship of island nations like Britain and imperial powers like the Hapsburgs, it's not much of a leap to understand why the events of 1914–1918 have gained, and deserve, the label "world war."

There tends to be a lot of textbook space devoted to these questions, which helps teachers frame the global contexts of the war. In part because

I am a historian of empire by training, and because empire is one of the recurrent global history themes of my syllabus, I'm especially interested in encouraging students to appreciate the imprint of imperialism on global histories (see chapter 7, "Empire as a Teaching Tool"). And so in the section of my syllabus devoted to the First World War I work hard to link nineteenth-century imperial unrest, interimperial competition, and global imperial anxieties to the story I tell. Until relatively recently, I did this pretty ham-handedly, by talking about big and small wars mainly in the British empire and especially during the South African War (1899–1900) and dramatizing how the outbreak of hostilities in 1914 and the conduct of war through the armistice might be viewed through a wider global lens. That expanded global narrative has variously included the Spanish American War and the Russo-Japanese wars, each of which has its deep and geopolitically far-reaching global genealogies, histories that are not necessarily self-evidently tethered to the First World War, but to which links, both allusive and taut, connective and divergent, can arguably be made. I'm motivated to do so as well by the desire to do more than mention that Indian troops helped defend the Alliance in the Somme and elsewhere: I want students to appreciate how the variety of bodies who died in battle or later from wounds, or who flooded European metropoles after the war and helped create multiracial societies of the twentieth century, got there in the first place, and how they shaped the outcomes of war. Rematerializing the imperial — the Asian, African, and circum-Caribbean — as well as the European backstage of the war allows students to see multiple frames of global history at once.[2] That backward glance can generate conversations and insights about origins, the processes of historical change, and, in this context, the very meaning of the term "world stage," with its privileging of "big" events, certain bodies, and dominant but naturalized perspectives. It can also move your narrative forward in multiple directions, as you track the afterlives of the tributaries you have made visible in the "rehearsal" of the war and its origins.

My own attempts to give some depth to the global origins of the First World War have been significantly enhanced by Isabel Hull's 2006 book, *Absolute Destruction*, which chronicles the German campaign against the

Herero in Southwest Africa in 1904–1907. Drawing on a variety of archival records and oral accounts, Hull reconstructs not simply the details of how and why the Germans pursued an annihilation order against the Herero, but the military culture from which it grew and from which, in turn, the German command drew lessons for the later larger war. Hull's claims that the routines "perfected in the colonies" were later used on European populations are controversial, especially insofar as they are linked to larger questions about the relationship between the Final Solution and imperial antecedents.[3] I don't take Hull's arguments at face value and, as I detail in chapter 8 ("Global Archive Stories"), I encourage students to look hard at the evidence Hull musters, to begin to assess the validity of her claims. I am content to leave the connections unresolved. At the end of discussion, I stake my position on the evidence and link it back to the larger narrative of global genealogies for the First World War that frames the readings more generally. I encourage students to think about the various tendrils and tributaries that might have contributed to the global character of the war and its cultures, returning at the end to the various battle fronts in order to map literally and visually the geopolitics of Axis-Alliance conflict. Last but not least, I refer students to W. E. B. DuBois's piece from 1915, "The African Roots of War," in which he famously argues that "in a very real sense Africa is a prime cause of this terrible overturning of civilization which we have lived to see; and these words seek to show how in the Dark Continent are hidden the roots, not simply of war to-day but of the menace of wars to-morrow."[4]

Textbooks can be helpful, as well as hindering, in cases like this. Not all perform the kinds of global maneuvers we might like; some may not even take genealogy or connectivity as a first principle. In such cases, you may need to be creative and encourage students to do the same. This may involve juxtaposing or combining different sections of the text in the same reading assignment, and directing students' attention to how events described in the imperialism section illuminate those found in the world war section. Such creative cuttings and pastings are almost always necessary when it comes to addressing women, gender, and sexuality, topics that may well be addressed in connection with a big event like war but may need amplification. So, for example, if you want to discuss women's suffrage in connection with the First World War, which makes sense given that the United States and Britain granted women of a certain age the vote in 1918–1920, you'd want to track the global genealogies of suffrage, including its origins as a successful legislative gambit in 1890s New Zealand. This gives you a chance to help students challenge their own U.S.-centrism and to ask where "modernity" happens. You would also want to be sure students get a sense of the vote's larger imperial remit and the uneven application of suffrage reform across the international spectrum, topics that reach backward into the nineteenth century and forward to the UN Declaration of Human Rights and, if you like, the Beijing Conference on Women (1995). These are hardly triumphalist narratives, given the long history of women's emancipation in imperial politics, the entanglement of suffrage with race and class hierarchies, and the long life of suffrage as a rationale for Western intervention in global wars down to the present day.

Although the example of modern warfare lends itself exceedingly well to the global genealogy method, there are myriad other examples that can be enlisted for this purpose as well. Commodities are a useful device here. I've already touched on the pedagogical value of tea and sugar for indexing the local and gendered workings of global imperial power (see chapter 4, "World History from Below"). And I have used silver to track early forms of global circulation (see chapter 2, "Centering Connectivity"). Each of these offers opportunities for a backstage look as well: tea and sugar through the global plantation complex and silver through the circulation of metals out of Japan, China, and Spanish America and into the Baltics, Russia, the Ottoman Empire, India, and the Pacific Ocean "via the Manila galleon to the Philippines."[5] Indigo, cochineal, coffee, rubber, fertilizer, cotton, cocaine have transnational histories and global pathways attached to them, even as they arrive at our sightline in the present shorn of those genealogical traces. Accounts of their pasts offer opportunities to bring questions of labor and the body to the fore in discussions of global capital, industrialization, credit, south-south relations, and even daily life. And attention to global commodity histories can cut across civilizational spaces, highlighting regional geographies enabled by production, consumption, and circulation, and underscoring the very specific moments in time when a global analysis is warranted for a particular space. Cotton, for example, operated in a kind of empire of its own, crisscrossing Britain, Brazil, the United States, and Japan, and in many ways defying any easy account of linear genealogy — which makes cotton a very useful indicator of the reciprocal impact of the local and the global. The genealogy of cotton allows students to appreciate why and how commodities help to make worlds in concrete terms.[6] Other examples might be enlisted to do different kinds of backstage work. Timothy Brook's lyrical invocation of Johannes Vermeer's painting *Woman Holding a Balance* (1664) elucidates the global genealogy of the silver coin on the table of Catharina, the model who was also Vermeer's wife, and gives students a powerful visual touchstone for the geopolitics of seventeenth-century Dutch currency. Brook's account gives students a way to imagine the complex, multinodal origins of middle-class European life and culture at what Brook calls "the dawn of the global world."[7] In Brook's able telling of the tale, we almost see the touch of the coin in Catharina's hand, and through that hand, the capillaries that lead out of the Netherlands and back into a deep history of cosmopolitan circuitry, through shipwrecks and massacres and the "percolation" of precious metal down to quotidian transactions that linked Europe to China, and to many spaces in between.[8] As a way to dramatize this, I like to juxtapose Vermeer's wife and her silver piece with a declarative line from a marriage song out of indigenous British Columbia: "I thought you were good. / I thought you were like silver; / you are lead."[9]

Because the seventeenth-century Dutch were not hyperconscious of their embeddedness in global genealogies, their insouciance is a pedagogical opportunity for us. I know several world history teachers who draft students into interactive classroom exercises to dramatize the global antecedents, in time and space, of commodities in the contemporary present. I call my version of this the "no sweat" routine, and I know many colleagues who do some version of it. I usually employ it in the section of my syllabus where I am dealing with the global histories of industrialization. It involves asking select students to part temporarily with a piece of clothing they are wearing — hats, gloves, shoes, etc. — which one of them deposits in a pile at the front of the room while another stands ready while I call out the "made in x" labels for him or her to list on the chalk board. The effect is to materialize how the shirts off students' backs come from disparate and distance places, and to drive home the commodity chains that help to produce their fashion and their daily raiment. I've also used Sweet Honey in the Rock's powerful song, "Are My Hands Clean?" as both a supplement to and a substitute for this exercise. The lyrics track the fictional pathway of a shirt from its origins of production in the southern hemisphere to the point of consumption in the northern hemisphere.[10] One of the many things I appreciate about the song is that it was written not from the promontory perspective of white liberal guilt but from the point of view of an African American woman, a working woman, caught up in a global genealogy she has not been an active agent in creating but in which she is also implicated. That haunting line — "Haiti, may she one day be free" — allows me to take students back through the twentieth-century history of the postcolonial and colonial Caribbean, to give a deep backstage to the Haitian earthquake and, however circuitously, to link earlier plantation histories to contemporary global conditions and struggles, to link them in ways that hopefully make visible the politics of location.

To these genealogical ends I also use the film *Life and Debt*, which cites Jamaica, and specifically its underemployed farm workers, and as a point of origin for twentieth-century global capitalization via the IMF and the World Bank. If I place these topics at the very end of my syllabus, they give me the chance to link these genealogies to current debates about microfinance and the Grameen Bank scheme, which privileges Third World women entrepreneurs under a new model of debt redemption, with all the millennial enthusiasms that entails. The touch of woman and coin that Vermeer's painting captures is perversely echoed here, as many students are familiar with Kiva.org, a global philanthropic site that allows those with some disposable income to "touch" the lives of non-Western women. As Ananya Roy, a sociologist of global poverty, has suggested, these are small stories with chains, literally and figuratively, that lead directly "up" from the so-called global bottom and from the recesses of the past, to world history subjects like global capital, global feminism, international politics, and, of course, "planetary" interdependence.[11] Perhaps unique among all the subjects on the syllabus, these genealogical questions animate and agitate students the most, in part because they resonate with other topics students encounter in an increasingly globalized (if not yet fully global) college and university curriculum. These questions are also evocative because they offer students the most practical grasp of the relationship between history as a kind of deep and spatial story and globalization as a historical phenomenon. At least that has been my experience. This is not to say that you should accept all the links I am trying to make or even the methodological skills, the history work, I am trying to suture into my lectures and class discussions. But looking backward, underneath, and behind is at least a start into debates over what place historical thinking can or should have in students' global education.

Chapter Seven

Empire as a Teaching Tool

Like a cyclone, imperialism spins across the globe . . .
KARL LIEBKNECHT

TRUE CONFESSIONS: my brief for empire as a strategy for teaching world history comes out of my training as a historian of the British empire and my experiences of teaching world history in various forms in two different public universities over the last twenty years. I suspect that most people who teach world history at the college and university level leave a trace of their own specialist knowledge on their syllabi, even if they are compelled to learn new bodies of literature, new conceptual models, and new ways of thinking about the domain of inquiry that the subject brings into view. Right out of graduate school in 1990, faced with two preparations for a term of world history a semester and feeling utterly overwhelmed by the prospect, I shaped my world history syllabi around imperialism because that was a template I was familiar with. It offered a spatial model for tracking all kinds of broad geographical connections; its core-periphery grid allowed for the integration of European histories with non-Western histories; and it enabled discussions of multiple scales of historical experience, contact, and exchange. And to be perfectly honest, using it as a design principle across the whole course helped to calm my muted panic at having to undertake such an intimidating pedagogical project, for which my graduate training did not prepare me at all. Though it's hard to imagine this now, almost all the terminology I would use today to rationalize this approach — transnationalism, contact zone, circulation, mobility, convergence, divergence, and connectivity, let alone the body as method — was unavailable as common currency then. In fact, world history was not the rage across curricula the way it has become in the last two decades (for that matter, neither was imperial history). My conviction about empire as a teaching tool has been fortified, in other words, by developments in each field and about the ways those fields have converged — unevenly and not without contest — in and around the field of global studies. Indeed, as I write, Jane Burbank and Frederick Cooper's book, *Empires in World History*, is hot off the press. In its opening pages, Burbank and Cooper argue that empire is a useful platform from which to access world history because "for most of human history empires and their interactions shaped the context in which people gauged their political possibilities, pursued their ambitions, and envisioned their societies. States large and small, rebels and loyalists, and people who cared little for politics — all had to take empires, their ways of rule, and their competitions into account."[1] Whether the purchase of this imperial framework still obtains, Burbank and Cooper conclude, is an open question.

After years of teaching and learning about world history, empire remains a critical teaching tool for me not simply because it resonates with my initial field of study, but because it has been, undeniably I think, one of the most salient modes by which "the world" was made global. Put another way, empire is a hard fact of world history, material evidence of the tracks that were laid to fulfill global ambitions on the part of numerous and variegated polities that experienced degrees of success and failure. Empires offer useful lessons about the possibilities of the global as a real and symbolic phenomenon. Using imperial power as a bright-line of world history allows students to grab on to what is, for better or worse, a recognizable set of systems through which to apprehend circuits of power, nodes of trade and exchange, interimperial rivalries, and, of course, resistance to and appropriation of all of the above by people for whom the benefits of empire were not intended. Empires illuminate how global systems emerged in historical terms. Though not necessarily or uniformly the cyclone of Liebknecht's imaginary, empires could have a tectonic effect on those who lived through them. And if their progenitors typically had totalizing ambition, their power was often halting and incomplete, even when it was deadly. In that sense, empires may be said to have worked in historical terms in the same way I have suggested that the global can work in pedagogical terms. Empires are a framework, a way of slicing temporal, spatial, and embodied histories that may or may not be connected. Whatever role you assign empire (and more on that below), you need to come to grips with it as an apparatus, though not the only one, that has helped to construct the world in historical, historiographical, and hence in pedagogical, terms.

One payoff of empire as a teaching tool is that by definition, its meanings are not fixed: they vary with the historically specific iterations of imperialisms across time and space. The Roman empire may have been the template for the British empire, and these empires may be usefully compared in many respects, but as a model, neither is transferrable to other historical forms of imperial arrangement. Depending on where you start your world history syllabus, in place or time, your working definition of empire will vary. And it will always allow you to take up related questions, like slavery, for example. As the work of James H. Sweet has shown, slaves in the diaspora of Portuguese imperialism facilitated the transfer of numerous practices — ritual, dietary, judicial — from Central Africa to Brazil that continue to shape the contemporary world.[2] Nor are empires per se distinct from the strategies by which they functioned. The "Asian" empires of the seventeenth century through the nineteenth (Romanov, Qing, Ottoman, and Mughal) were more centrally coordinated than, say, European, oceanic empires. This central coordination had ramifications for how these empires prospered and failed and for their status as models of despotism and absolutism, as well as for empire tout court. Even grouping the Romanovs in this set is an interesting move; among other things, it suggests how useful startling combinations and juxtapositions of imperial forms can be for developing analytical and comparative skills, and, in this case, for determining the boundaries of Asia in any given time and place. The science writer Steven Johnson calls this the power of the "adjacent possible," suggesting that it allows scientists to see and think in recombinant ways.[3] For our purposes, the pressure of a world history context offers new configurations and forces us to ask hard questions about likeness and dissimilarity and about our standards of evidence and argumentation for both. As Trevor Getz and Heather Streets-Salter have argued, the very designations "empire" and "imperial" must be made with care, in part because of the presumption that modern Western imperial forms can be read backwards onto early or even contemporaneous forms. The terms themselves tend to flatten out internal complexities and contradictory historical forces, such as the differences between informal empire and settler colonialism.[4]

In my own syllabus, I use empire as part of the architecture of the course in order to have a consistent but flexible frame inside which to organize diverse materials and create a chronological momentum. I wish I could be less wedded to the latter, and when I've taught world histories at levels of the curriculum beyond the 100, I work much more thematically. But I have found that in the introductory course, where I have up to 225 students and may or may not have TAs to lead small discussions, a fairly conventional forward-moving narrative (in my case, c. 1300–present) is necessary for getting and keeping students' attention (it's no guarantee, of course, but it's one less battleground). In this setting, empire serves as a metanarrative device, allowing me to track common themes, draw spatial boundaries around vast and mainly unfamiliar terrains of the globe, and suggest comparisons between imperial projects across time and space. So, for example, I juxtapose my lecture on British imperialism with one on the Russian empire, a field I have become an avid reader in because of its Eurasian, North American, and Arctic histories—histories that force me to think of the Raj and other British dominions as less spatially bounded, histories that throw me and my students into questions of environment and indigenous culture. These, together with the efflorescence of work on the ocean worlds of global history, have pushed me to think of western imperial power as shaped as much by littorals and salty seas as by boots on the ground.[5] I tend to absorb American histories into an imperial framework, linking the Comanche empire to the Mongol through horses (see chapter 2, "Timing: Where to Begin") and using the complex of wars (Spanish American, Philippine, Russo-Japanese, and South African) as an opportunity to talk about a significant shift in geopolitics on the threshold of the twentieth century—a so-called American century that emerged out of multiple imperial entanglements and complexly global antecedents. Indeed, given its inspiration for nationalists like Jawaharlal Nehru, historians have begun to ask why the twentieth century doesn't begin with the Russo-Japanese War.[6] That war left a deep cleft in several places, giving rise in the short and long term to Japanese imperialism in Manchuria, sedimenting a "blood claim" to it for post-1905 generations. The war can also be understood as a "global anti-western moment" that launched a variety of modernities, Asian modernities included.[7]

Keeping the question of resistance to empire alive as part of the history of global power is also a priority for me. Here, recurrent attention to world history from below (see chapter 4) proves useful: not only can I center the struggle over imperial power but I can also offer examples of how and when imperial power was unstably gained and unstably held in the face of labor agitation, anticolonialism, or everyday challenges to colonial rule.[8] Needless to say, each of these subjects can be driven by the body, by a "world history from below" angle, or both. I use the image of the Filipina breast—an icon of American imperial notions of colonial savagery—to anchor my treatment of the U.S. fin-de-siècle "savage wars of peace." In so doing, I return students to an essay we've read earlier in the course about early modern travelers' preoccupation with African women's breasts to try to create an embodied arc of imperial imagery across very disparate yet related times and places.[9] Nor is this kind of connective maneuver only possible for modern empires, as Burbank and Cooper's pairing of Rome and China show. Contrasting images of a Roman arch and a Chinese wall, Burbank and Cooper take fragmentary evidence and use it as the basis for a set of reflections on the commonalities and distinctions between the two.[10] My own comparative staple involves the court of Suleiman the Magnificent (1494–1566) and that of Louis XIV (1638–1715). I use this pairing to underscore the presence of two imperially minded monarchs whose territorial ambitions were unquestionably global in the premodern era. I make the case for this quite factually, noting how each expanded the territorial reach of their states and saw themselves as patrons of the arts as well. Absolute monarchs both, Suleiman and Louis XIV exercised imperial power that was dependent on and consolidated by their cultural aspirations, aspirations which in turn were vested in the bodies of each royal person—a point I embellish with portraiture and other details that make connections between the empire and the imperial body politic.

I could of course go into far greater detail about these two men—and this, as we know, is the great temptation of world history: the welter of fabulous detail. But here, as in the lecture, I want to emphasize what the comparison of these two imperial figures can do for students. First, it enables them to see two sovereigns in two different centuries who built and defended political regimes with tentacles well beyond the immediate geographies of their personal rule. Second, it makes clear that such regimes were carriers of systems of taxation, of language, and of cultural forms that impacted the high political fates of nations and everyday life on the ground well beyond their capital cities. Third, it requires us to consider the incredible complexity of geopolitics and territorial ambition before the onset of modernity, which I think many students tend to view as the original moment of empires and global interconnectedness. And last but not least, it compels us to recognize that what we think of as Western forms of political power and worldly ambition were actually not unique to the West—put another way, if we look at the world with the Ottoman empire at the center in this period, rather than France or Europe, we get a sense of how unexceptional Louis XIV was in terms of his quest for power and his geopolitical accomplishments. Could I achieve all these points without empire as the grounds of comparison? Very probably. But placing the comparison in that imperial frame allows me to draw students into earlier lecture examples of, say, embodied imperial power (the Qing emperor, for instance, whose robes and palace setting I've already read for similar meanings) and to project forward to Queen Victoria for the nineteenth century and Hirohito for the mid-twentieth century. I try here and elsewhere to use empire as both a tight and a loose framework. Suleiman and Louis XIV were not exactly contemporaries; their empires had different contours and very different fates. How legitimate is this comparison? On what argumentative and evidentiary basis do I make it? These are questions I ask aloud and also test students on (see chapter 10, "Testing (for) the Global"). In doing so, I draw heavily on the work of Suraiya Faroqhi, who argues that "in the sixteenth and seventeenth centuries, Ottomans and Frenchmen . . . were less remote from one another than the people under study themselves would have thought." She uses this contention to make a case for the Ottoman empire as its own world economy, and this is yet another way to move from empire to the global and back again.[11] Such comparisons and observations are not only possible using empire, but if empire is part of the course design, they may have more pedagogical effect.

Another mechanism of comparison is, of course, to "think" empires comparatively, outside examples from the West. Any number of textbooks juxtapose the Ottomans, the Safavids, and the Mughals precisely to dramatize their shared temporality, their parallels with and distinctiveness from contemporary European models, and even to track the traffic between them. Empires are a useful tool, then, for identifying patterns and thinking about processes of pattern-making. With their webs and networks and capillaries of power, they are also good examples of interconnectivity. In my own teaching and writing career, I have been especially invested in using empires as a way of puncturing the supposed insularity of Western nation-states — in tracking historical examples of how, in Frantz Fanon's words, "Europe [is] the invention of the third world."[12] So my syllabus section on modern imperialism is devoted in part to enabling students to appreciate how imperialism did not only move outward from London to, say, Calcutta or Cape Town, but how frequently those colonial spaces "blew back" people, ideas, goods, and histories that in turn shaped what "domestic" Britain looked like. In a direct echo of my lecture on 1492, I open my remarks on "empire at home" with a passage and an image from the museum catalog *Spain in the Age of Exploration*, which describes how images of the Incan emperor Atahualpa and the Mexican emperor Montezuma are to be found on the doors of the royal palace in Madrid, side by side with those of the Spanish kings and the heart of the Iberian empire.[13] I recap earlier lectures in which I laid out empire as an outward expansion from a center, such as Rome and London, to "peripheries," such as Gaul and India. I review the vectors of West and East and the rhetoric of the "gift" of civilization and uplift from center to periphery. As a counterpoint to empire as territorial expansion, I offer a telescoped account of how Britain at home was made in part through its colonial possessions since the sixteenth century. International slavery — which with monopoly capitalism was "the spinal cord" of modern Western commercial prosperity — brought gold, ivory, pepper, and even some slaves to English shores. The Tudors and Stuarts had "blackamoors" at their courts, men and women of African and Indian descent populated the streets of Georgian London, and provincial lives were both full of and economically dependent on the raw materials extracted from Britain's colonies.[14] During the Victorian era, evidence of Britain's imperial wealth and power continued to make its way to the heart of the empire in the form of human and commercial capital, as the traffic in goods and people from the colonies became crucial to Britain's national and international preeminence in the modern period. One simple and commonplace example of the impact of empire on domestic British society is to be found in the word "guinea." By the eighteenth century, "guinea" was the popular name for the coin struck from gold, the coin in which servants were paid their wages. The gold originated on the coast of Africa, where the coin got its name. And so on.[15]

If this kind of example works out, students have a number of different models of empire throughout world history, and narratives that plot them from different angles: above and below, micro and macro, embodied and chillingly abstract. What students also have, ideally, is the beginning of a capacity to distinguish between different imperial forms and between different imperial projects. Here the juxtaposition of empires (British and Chinese during the Opium Wars), the way they compete with each other (Dutch and British in Southern Africa), the way they mimic each other (Russians looking to Paris as well as London), and the way they meet up uneasily in commercial and strictly territorial terms (Russians, British, French, and Chinese in Tianjin) can be useful for getting at how linkages between and across varied imperial phenomena might work.[16] I'm sensitive, of course, to the politics of a British empire model that organizes world history. Britain is one empire, and it does not the world make, despite the fiction about this link that Victorians and those who have come after have often been prepared to accept. In the last ten years, I have had to educate myself in the histories of other imperial powers, precisely in order to avoid that tender trap. For me, studying empire is an ongoing process of rethinking and retraining. The challenge here is one of proportionality, both with respect to the amount of British empire material I rely on and with respect to the role of empire as a conceptual tool for the course as a whole. Empires can obscure as much as they reveal; they can privilege a top-down view and they can calcify polities into sovereign subjects, when in fact fluidity, porousness, and even failed hegemony may have actually been the modus operandi. As with many such devices, what's advantageous about empire is also disadvantageous: empire runs the risk of looking coherent and bundled up, when history, and especially world history, is rarely, if ever, that neat. So not every session in my syllabus deals with or even alludes to empire, in part because empire is just one of three thematic devices that structure the syllabus. The other two — the worlds that trade has made and the work of women, gender, and the body — sometimes work in service of an empire analytic, but not always. And because I stage some topics on the syllabus in which I have very little expertise, I invite colleagues to come in as guest lecturers, a practice that can either enhance or dilute my best-laid thematic plans. If you teach in the kind of institution where it's possible to host guest lecturers, I recommend at least a few specialist lectures, not least because they can model how to do a given topic. Guest experts compel you to take material not your own and thread it imaginatively through your own design templates — a process that illuminates that design very clearly to you and allows you to draw attention to how it fits your own model and how it doesn't as well.

Empire is, in the end, one mode of globality and one model for thinking the global, but it's by no means the only one. As teachers of world history, we have to grapple with empire and we have to decide for ourselves what its proportional explanatory role is in our arguments about how world histories have been and should be made. If empire is not one of your bright-lines, what do you use to illuminate the global pathways that your course aims to materialize for students interested in acquiring knowledge about the world's pasts and skills for deciphering its presents and futures? From where I sit, such presents and futures would seem to be entangled in empires of all kinds.

PART III

Teaching Technologies

HERE I PROPOSE a variety of technologies—by which I mean delivery systems for both content and critical historical thinking skills—for enabling students to be hyperaware of the pressure of time and place on the way they access the past. How is our access to world history mediated by a variety of things: the digital world, archival sources, and historians' interpretations? And how can we as teachers use assignments and exams to make sure that our evaluative tools, our diagnostics, are encouraging a variety of forms of critical global-history thinking?

---- *Chapter Eight* ----

Teaching "Digital Natives"

ANYONE BORN AFTER 1980 is a "digital native," and anyone born before that date is a "digital immigrant." What dis-
tinguishes the two generations is their relationship to social
media. The "natives" spend much of their life online; they
don't draw sharp distinctions between their virtual and actual
identities; and they have created "a 24/7 network that blends
the human with the technical to a degree that we haven't experienced before." They haven't known "anything but a life
connected to one another, and to the world of bits" that, in
turn, plugs them in to "friends all over the world." Most significantly, "this culture is global in scope and nature." The information superhighway that is the World Wide Web is part of a
"global culture" and it's a story "that is breaking all around us,
at unprecedented speed." We're either in or out—consigned
to a primitive, predigital past or embracing "a bright future in
a digital age."[1]

With any luck, this simplistic paradigm—which I've drawn
directly from John Palfrey and Urs Gasser's runaway bestseller,

Born Digital: Understanding the First Generation of Digital Natives — is not your model for globalization or global history. Even if it is, it need not be your model for teaching to a digital-savvy, even digital-addicted, classroom of teenagers and twenty-somethings or for using technology as a teaching tool, either. No one can dispute the impact of new technological forms on all aspects of social, political, and economic life, at least in the prosperous West — and not even always there, a point to which I shall return. And while we are still in the first generation of research on the impact of new digital technologies on cognitive processes and learning, it would be folly to gainsay the role of digital media and all its virtual forms in enhancing students' access to information, if not their critical skills and capacity for learning. To deny this would be to ignore a basic fact of educational curricula at almost any level; namely, that in less than a decade, Wikipedia alone has "singlehandedly invigorated and disrupted" the world of the encyclopedia — thrusting that Enlightenment paean to universal knowledge into a whole new set of dimensions and a radically expanded audience of readers and consumers.[2] Even more to the point for our purposes, as Andrew Lih has observed, "in the English Wikipedia, where activity is non-stop, articles have become an instant snapshot of the state of the world, serving as a continuous working draft of history."[3]

Yet if you are anything like me, you may find this fact to be a combination of exhilarating and overwhelming — something akin to what some of us experience when we contemplate the very prospect of teaching a world history course. One solution to this muted panic is to return to first principles: to ask, what are the takeaways I hope students will leave the course with — both in terms of content and ways of seeing — and what are the most effective ways of achieving, if not ensuring, that students get what I am aiming for? Digital technology, whatever its form, should function the same way that a textbook or primary-source reader or even the architecture of your syllabus does: it's not an end in itself but a delivery system for knowledge and skill-building that dovetails with your arguments about the nature, scope, and history of the global. Like the readings you choose and the themes you nominate, you are always engaged in processes of case-making and experimentation that are authoritative but also provisional, processes subject to discussion and querying in ways that model for students various examples of "fact" and theory, evidence and argument, in a global context. If, in other words, your case for this timeframe or that, this model of interconnectivity versus that one, is part of the experience of grappling with history and "the world," so too your use of digital tools merits direct address in the classroom as part of the larger problem of world history itself.

Some self-disclosure is in order here. By Palfrey and Gasser's calculations, I am a digital immigrant rather than a digital native and as such (in their view) I may have one foot in the digital world but I will never understand it from the inside, as a native would. Never mind that the labels "immigrant" and "native" are politically and ideologically loaded, positing transhistorical essences and divides of the kind that cannot apparently be crossed — and which my approach to the world as a historian invested in the contingency and dynamism of all historical forms and phenomena would seem to be in direct conflict with. Moreover, I am committed to teaching world history in part because I am interested in helping to equip students with a skepticism about the newness of the global and about its teleological claims — the very kind of juggernaut mentality that seems to drive the whole digital native thesis and to render us all passive, or at the very least reactive, objects of its inevitability.

Ideally your approach to the digital as a teaching tool is as thought through and planned for as any other part of your syllabus. Because my own approach to the introductory level of world history is rooted in a set of convictions about the capacity of historical methods to unpick the times, spaces, and scales of the global, I take my cue from Richard White, a historian of the American West (broadly speaking) and director of Stanford University's Spatial History Project. This research consortium uses computer modeling to organize data into a variety of spatial forms — graphs, tables, and maps, to name a few — and thus to enhance our understanding of what he calls "visual evidence." The Stanford website offers many fascinating and eminently teachable examples of this technological wizardry, and anyone with an internet connection and sufficient broadband capacity can get to it. For a quick but instructive look at how this works, I recommend you go to "Aaron Koblin's Flight Patterns" and "Napoleon's March by Joseph Millard," which may be among the most useful examples of this process for world history purposes. As important is White's emphasis on such models as instruments in the service of historical questions and methodological approaches, even he and his coinvestigators take note of how those questions and approaches; may change under the pressure of new technological capabilities. He resists the notion of technological revolution or paradigm shift in the Kuhnian sense, urging a sense of proportionality and even modesty when it comes to the application of digital tools to historical evidence and thinking. "I think what we are doing is different," he says of the Spatial History Project, "but we are not announcing the end of history as you know it or of the text or of the narrative. Historians will continue to write books. Historians will continue to tell stories."[4] Or as Robert Darnton, speaking of the apparent collision of the book with new social media, and drawing on his knowledge of the history of communication, observes: "One medium does not displace another, at least not in the short run."[5]

Having said that, we do need to grab — and keep — students' attention and speak in terms that are relevant to them if we want to harness their imaginations to the power of history. Having said *that*, and despite the often glib assumption that internet access is a "global" phenomenon, the availability of digital resources is uneven across the United States, contingent not just on the extant funding to buy software and hardware but on the capacity of schools, colleges, and universities to get their infrastructures up to speed. Access is also dependent on their willingness to choose technology over other pressing needs in an era of scarce resources. In this context, PowerPoint is likely the most accessible and user-friendly medium; many textbooks come equipped with e-files with content and images that can be incorporated into a lecture; and dual screens, if you can get them, can enhance comparisons of space and place, and enhance the cross-referencing of textual and visual clues to a larger lecture or discussion questions about connection, trade links, maps, and the like. For the benefit of the so-called tech-fascinated we teach, there are a variety of "clicker" options: tools for setting up multiple-choice questions and adding up student responses as a jumping off point for further elaboration. And if you have a live internet connection in your classroom, the possibilities are endless. You can call up all manner of sites and images, access databases that can materialize anything from Marco Polo's *Travels* to the vast, if not entire, corpus of the website Early English Books Online. You can trawl through the textual worlds such sites throw up, exposing students to poems and prescriptive literature, to histories both famous and obscure — often in crystal clear facsimile, which can be a breathtaking experience for teacher and pupil alike. For students who only use Twitter or Facebook, even such basic exercises may, literally and figuratively, open up worlds for them they had no clue existed, worlds they can easily explore themselves. As any teacher in this century knows, there are pleasures and perils to this embarrassment of digital riches. Caveat emptor: you had better have your school's plagiarism policy on the syllabus and you had better have an express discussion of how to cite from the web — not because all students are potential plagiarizers but because in the 24/7 networked world they travel in, the difference between what is "public and general" knowledge and what needs attribution is often unclear, to say the least.

And as anyone who has surfed the web knows only too well, the vast quantities of information available have to be processed, understood, and critically evaluated — challenges for all history teachers, regardless of subject matter. In fact, the creative use of digital history tools and materials can actually dramatize the "where do we see it from" question that underlies world history as a project, insofar as digital technology clearly mediates — by bundling, plotting, and arranging — the "information" we have about the global past more dramatically, more performatively even for a born-digital generation, than the book may be seen to do. So if you use PowerPoint slides to compare an Iberian map of the world with a Mayan or Incan one from the same period, side by side on an overhead screen, you have an opportunity for shared and simultaneous viewing that is worthy of comment: it's a positionality that no contemporary Spaniard or Incan would likely have had in common and it offers a chance to talk about the limits and possibilities of a "Columbian" world view. Similarly, if you throw a document like Rudyard Kipling's famous 1899 poem, "The White Man's Burden," into the website Wordle—which will produce a beautiful word cloud showing the most commonly recurrent words in a scaled pattern—you have a chance to talk visually, as it were, about what Kipling's view of Anglo-American empire "looked" like, or how "worldly" it is in terms of the diversity of its national or geographical referents. And there's no denying that Geographic Information Systems (GIS) platforms have the power to map time and spaces in new forms and, literally, in multiple dimensions.[6] Meanwhile, if all my lectures could be converted into RSA Animate form—whereby what you say is turned into a still cartoon with word bubbles and annotation—I'd be in heaven.

These are not substitutes for other kinds of reading or learning material, of course. They are what Michael Michalko helpfully calls "thinker-toys": technologies that do not *create* history, but *suggest* creative ways of both apprehending it and appreciating it in new ways.[7] And they remind us that the relationship of technology to technique is not merely semantic. Technologies are specific techniques (methods, mechanisms, and delivery systems), only some of which are digital. Take the work of the Beehive Design Collective, a group located in eastern Maine that has developed strategies of graphic and visual communication you can fold directly into a lecture or discussion section. Of particular interest might be their "Plan Colombia" graphic, the result of oral histories they did in Colombia and Ecuador that represents 500 years of Latin American history, linking "first colonization" to drug wars and forms of militarization that have arisen in our own time. It's one of a series of images that enables students to see how time and space "cross-pollinate" in the context of global history.[8] When I tell you that this kind of technology pushes me way beyond my comfort zone, I do not exaggerate. It forces me to face my logocentricity and learn new ways of seeing and talking about history and the global that are very, very humbling, though exciting as well.

The Beehive Design Collective has a web archive, one of millions of websites you can use in your course to dramatize the global in multiple ways. It's available in both English and Spanish. For the purposes of world history, remember that the digital world, in all its vastness, is but a partial archive, created in part via the machinery of transnational capital and heavily biased in favor of English-language sources. If your students are predominantly English speakers, this may not be a problem, but this bias also serves as a reminder, to you and to them, of the limits of the digital world for accessing global history beyond certain quite narrow linguistic parameters. If your students are not English speakers, this bias allows all kinds of avenues into conversations about the limits and possibilities of "global English" and of global history textbooks written in the United States. Meanwhile, if you are looking for specific exercises or approaches to teaching world history modules, I can recommend "World History Connected," an ungated site that is subtitled "The E-Journal of Learning and Teaching" and funded in part by the College Board.[9] A mix of scholarly and pedagogical material, it's a treasure trove of debate, book reviews, and hands-on teaching resources that many of you reading this primer will likely already be familiar with if you have even dipped your toe into the internet world of world history. There really is something for everyone there — whether an established middle school teacher or a brand new PhD staring down a world history assignment — including ongoing debate about pressing current educational issues like the recent revisions of the AP World History exam.

If you are a Google-maniac like me, you know that lesson plans abound on the net. Just type "Bengal and Jamestown" and you get a step-by-step outline of how to compare these early British colonial "settlements."[10] But a word of warning here: not only are digital resources partial, they can have very short lives, which is why I have resisted the temptation to produce a slew of URLs here. IT folks call this "link rot," and it's an occupational hazard for digital natives and immigrants alike: another instructive reminder of the fleetingness and changeability of history, that of the web included. I try to make this a refrain of the course, not least because it's a way of getting students to appreciate their own historical placement in global and technological terms simultaneously. Students should imagine a world and a time when they might be worthy of the moniker "digital primitives," and in the not too distant future at that.

I have opted not to call this chapter "Teaching with Technology" but rather, "Teaching 'Digital Natives,'" and that's by design. In the first instance, "digital history sources" — of which White's project and the EEBO, mentioned above, are both examples — can be a misleading term. For while "digital" suggests a virtual or online source, those sources are often, if not most often, still textual in nature; indeed, the textuality of the digital sphere is as relentless as it is unremarked upon, ironically in an age of anxiety about the disappearance of the traditional book. The Kindle and the iPad both do so much to mimic that form — in content and readability, in feel and look — that the divide between the two is surely exaggerated. Or the divide is a difference of degree, rather than kind. For our purposes, it's worth noting that writing — whether in blogs, online posting sites, or traditional papers and exams — is still considered by educators to be essential, indispensable even, to historical thinking, if not critical thinking more generally. As Erik Vincent has observed, the range of options here is wide: from conventional papers to journaling to free-writes; each can support the fact-interpretation nexus and, in ways that give some students a charge, underscoring the detective element of the historian's process.[11] Lynn Hunt, former president of the American Historical Association, has been even more eloquent: "Writing means many different things to me but one thing it is not: writing is not the transcription of thoughts already consciously present in my mind. Writing is a magical and mysterious process that makes it possible to think differently."[12]

As Jaron Lanier, author of *You Are Not a Gadget*, suggests, the jury is still out on whether the digital classroom enhances or enfeebles the mind.[13] Nor should we make facile assumptions about what our students, those digital mavens, want or value. In an article entitled "Classes No Longer 'Paper-ful' Due to Internet Classwork" in the student newspaper at the University of Illinois, a freshman wrote:

> By forfeiting their right to teach students face-to-face, professors who rely heavily on online-based coursework are giving us an easy out for our education. And even though we may not need to know half of the stuff we are being taught in our general education requirements, when we leave this place behind, it is not about that.

It is about principality over probability; retaining something rather than memorizing it . . . My History . . . professor [Harry Liebersohn] is often dismayed and slightly saddened by the lack of attendance at his lectures because he has something worth saying, and many students skip out before even giving him a chance say it. But I guess it's their loss. By attending his lectures I learn something the textbook and PowerPoint cannot teach. I get a perspective that goes beyond dates and facts. He tells a story through his lectures, and it is evident to me that the presence and passion with which he teaches has something more to say than the PowerPoint slides he creates.[14]

This student and others like her are bemoaning what scientists call the "second-order effects" of technological innovation, effects "rarely captured by forecasts, laboratory experiments . . . [and] white papers," or, we might add, by university structures galloping to innovate via digital and social media.[15] Old and new media have, of course, been colliding for centuries, and life in our own time is no different. The media scholar Henry Jenkins calls this "convergence culture," and though he means it to evoke the circulation of media content across different systems, the relationship between reading and writing — by hand or by text — is an important part of these dynamic questions, with which history as a profession must grapple as new media shapes us and we shape it in the process.[16] Has the revolution in social media and its delivery systems produced a shift from intensive to extensive reading habits among digital natives?[17] And if so, what is the best way to cultivate critical, historical thinking and writing and skills in its wake?

I'll have more to say on writing about world history in chapter 10 ("Testing (for) the Global"). For now, I'd like to focus on the enduring benefits of another, ostensibly old-fashioned technology, in-person classroom pedagogy, for cultivating not just critical global thinking but confidence in thinking, and especially speaking, knowledgeably in a world history classroom setting. For I do believe that in an age of heightened digital media and a historical moment of often total exposure to it, students need as much embodied pedagogy as they do the virtual kind, or at least some combination of the two.

I teach my intro-level course to between 150 and 225 students — not the biggest university classroom setting imaginable, but big enough. And the seats are nailed to the floor, which forces me into a stand-and-deliver mode I am not especially a fan of, but which there is little way around. I use an interactive course system (or "academic suite") for posting assignments, lecture outlines, study guides, and test preparation. When I teach with TAs, students have two lectures a week and an hour of discussion section. But I am a firm believer in the possibility of discussion even in a big lecture forum. So I use a technique called "the Hot Seat," which was developed by my colleague Fred Hoxie and has also been used by my colleague Kristin Hoganson, in whose class I first observed it. This is an exercise that begins as a question-and-answer session and, when successful, turns into a fulcrum for debate on some part or parts of the material connected to the reading and lecture for the day.

Most importantly, the Hot Seat is a regular feature of the course: students rotate into it every session by sitting in seats at the front of the room. They know what texts they will be asked questions of ahead of time and I work to integrate their answers back into the larger themes and purposes of the day. Hot Seat days are marked on the syllabus. I don't do it every session, but it happens in about half the lectures of the semester. I e-mail questions to students and TAs ahead of time, allowing TAs to help students grasp the questions and prep for the in-class exchange. I ask students the questions at the start of the class. I do back and forth with students for as long as I can, working to draw them out and, at the same time, deeper into the material by pressing them past their first, often monosyllabic, answer. I reference the questions and their responses in my lecture. I follow up with e-mail and invite students to office hours to continue the conversation or to touch base about the course. I get about a 50 percent yield there; but TAs have said it helped get those students involved and talking in section, too.

My questions start empirically, rooted in the reading for the day. So, for example, beginning questions might include, "What is the most remarkable of Zheng He's accomplishments?" and "Why did the Chinese curtail the voyages of mariners like him? What were the historical consequences of this decision?" Many textbooks have such questions at the ends of chapters, and you can profitably draw on them. But keep in mind your purpose for doing so. Mine includes a commitment to helping students prepare well for class—for lecture, in my case—and instructing them via the pre-sent questions how to read for detail and for interpretive *connections*: the building blocks of historical thinking. Not incidentally, the Hot Seat enables me to learn students' names and get to know them; and it gives them a chance to shape what the lecture is about with their responses.

As with all the other design principles in this primer, I use the Hot Seat as one of several overall course objectives. These include (1) creating and sustaining intellectual investment and buy-in, (2) breaking down the macro into the micro, (3) learning to recognize interconnectedness and comparison as a set of skills, as well as simply a "topic," (4) building from the specific to the general, and (5) cultivating interpretive skills that privilege global thinking. These goals are absolutely possible to achieve, even in a big course. Indeed, I talk about them openly when I explain the Hot Seat at the start of the semester, when I use it to start a class session and especially if and when the student comes to see me afterwards. That latter interaction, that one-on-one encounter, can lead the student to have the courage to answer a question in lecture when she's not in the Hot Seat, and she may even come to office hours in advance of an exam to get preparation help. I can think of more than a few students whose grades have raised from Cs to Bs as a direct result of contact with me or the TA in the wake of a Hot Seat experience. The grade is not as important to me as it is to them; and naturally it's very important to them. If the Hot Seat closes the gap between my podium and their feeling of proximity to the material, it has done more than I ever intended. And in an age of ubiquitous social media, closing that gap may well be a new form of radical pedagogical intimacy.[18]

Big courses are not, of course, intimidating by definition; and, to be sure, many students take big courses precisely to be anonymous. Yet even when world history is taught in a small classroom its "bigness" can be scary. I attend to these questions because the bigness of world history, combined with the bigness and impersonality of a large lecture course, can obscure the personhood, the embodied experience, of the student. It can even make her seem microscopic, both to you and in the scheme of things. Such obstacles to an interactive learning experience can be overcome, but they have to be built into the course design. No matter what techniques you use, whether digital or more personally interactive, they have to be a regular feature of your syllabus; they have to be, in other words, a design principle of the larger pedagogical enterprise — tools we use "to bend the ... course of technology to meet our own."[19] In that sense, the digital does not have a monopoly on the category "technology." It's one of many methods for cultivating global thinking in a historical frame.

Chapter Nine

Global Archive Stories

BEFORE THE RISE OF HISTORY as a profession in the West, the footnote was a masterpiece of both art and design. In Edward Gibbon's *History of the Decline and Fall of the Roman Empire*, some of the most scandalous details and entertaining passages were relegated to the bottom of the page. As Anthony Grafton has so engagingly observed, Gibbon could "invest a bibliographic citation with the grave symmetry of a Ciceronian peroration . . . he could supply a comic parallel . . . and he could salute earlier scholars . . . with a unique combination of amused dismissal . . . and genuine respect." Gibbon was completely aware of his capacity for subtextual melodrama: he saw it as a positive feature of his *History*. He suggested that a comprehensive account of his sources was "susceptible of entertainment as well as information."[1] And as Grafton makes clear, the work of historical interpretation also went on in Gibbon's footnotes. Though the lay reader may see those footnotes as a by-product of the historian's process — Grafton goes so far as to say they might even be read as "waste-products" — and we as teachers may consider them too detailed or eso-teric for entry-level undergraduates to be concerned with, they are in fact an invaluable teaching tool, and nowhere more so, perhaps, than in world history.

Footnotes are like a breadcrumb trail: they lead us back from a claim about processes and events, a claim that may be synthesized from several sources, primary and secondary. In that sense they offer an opportunity to model the kind of tracking or genealogical work students of history can and should be aware of, so that they can do it themselves. History is the art and science of induction — building up from the ground, assessing evidence piece by piece, sifting, selecting, and accounting for what makes a persuasive case and even what contradicts it. When you ask students to scour the footnotes you are asking them to engage in a similar process. Just using the term "footnote" can be an aid to opening up broader conversa-tions about proof and argument and the other disciplinary conventions that shape them. Looking at the footnotes also allows us to see where the author has obtained her information and how she has derived her inter-pretation. Depending on the character and quality of the notation, stu-dents can sometimes evaluate the credibility of a claim. They can assess the type or quantity of sources cited, and depending on the level of the course and the availability of the original document or text, they can go and look for themselves to see if the claim can legitimately be drawn from it. Needless to say, getting students knee-deep in footnotes as a recurrent feature of your course makes conversations about authorship, originality, and plagiarism commonplace. It doesn't prevent plagiarism, but it means that when borrowing or outright copying does occur you have a broader context of practice to refer back to as you make your point about the need for proper attribution as a technical necessity and a responsible practice.

In a world history syllabus, even at the introductory level, it's both pos-sible and desirable to engage in these kinds of conversations. When I work with TAs, some of this can happen in discussion section, via the primary sources that are a staple of all introductory-level syllabi, world or not. But I also site conversations about sources, and more specifically about archives, in my lectures and in a variety of exercises I can do from the lectern. I have several aims in mind here, beyond exposing students to some basic archive talk. First, I want to encourage them to be more scrupulous readers, to look beyond the sightline of the assigned word and seek out the backstage, the material that helped produce the source. Second, I want them to bring their burgeoning global-history thinking skills to bear on texts and footnotes. I want students to see how historians track circulation and mobility, on what basis they claim that "exchange" occurred or that trade was global, and how exactly—which is to say, by what means and methods—historians read for and evaluate the global in their work. On this point, I make a direct connection between historians' capacity to think globally and the student's own, not simply to draw the student into "the craft" but to underscore the porous membrane that separates her from the community of historians: students too can do this work, and as they learn to do it they can learn from a variety of models that may be more or less successful at capturing globality, depending on what our standards are. Last but not least, I try to impress upon them the huge challenges facing students of the past, regardless of discipline or method, when it comes to knowing, with any kind of totality or certainty, what happened and why. This leads from a notion of archives as partial and selective and to a notion of "the archive" as flexible and elastic. This approach operates as well from the presumption that archives tell stories, and that archives *are always already* stories—they have narratives, both intrinsic and contingent, both extractable and deeply interred, that impact how historians see what they see and what they settle or unsettle in terms of the accounts they then write as "history."[2]

I've had success in these endeavors by teaching with excerpts from two historical monographs built into the reading of my world history syllabus. The first is from Marcus Rediker's *The Slave Ship*, which students read in the context of a session called "Maritime Empires and the Global System of Slavery."[3] I enter into a discussion of arguments and archives via the Hot Seat, an exercise in which I ask a preestablished group of several students, who sit at the front of the class, to answer some preset questions about the reading (for details on the concept, see chapter 8, "Teaching 'Digital Natives'"). I use the ship as a way to transition from demographics to bodies, and to ask what we get when we focus, as Rediker does in the chapter we read, on the captain. How, in prosaic terms, does Rediker break it down? What does a history of the captain buy us? We appreciate his ship-board authority, certainly, but we also get some insight into his strategic position in a "rapidly expanding international capitalist economy." Focusing on specific quotes from the text itself, we walk through other dimensions of the shipboard experience that are accessible via the sources on the captain: his role in meting out state-licensed corporal punishment, his skills and technical knowledge as a craftsman, his overriding function as a boss over wage labor (white and black) and as a manager of property. We pull out evidence of his relationship to merchant capital, his responsibility for micromanaging the voyage and the pathways he offers into merchant fears — desertion, suicide, and slave mortality — and his own fears as well. In each case I am asking students to mine the reading, which I hope they have a copy of before them (I don't project this one overhead; I want them to either have it in front of them or figure out that they need to for next time). I am asking them to treat Rediker's prose as a first layer of archive. As such, our first destination is his claim that "the very fragility of power aboard the ship may have increased its ruthlessness."

Does Rediker prove his case? On what basis? Rediker's chapter is helpfully broken into sections that structure my own journey through the argument and the sources. He uses, as well, a rich variety of sources, from ship records to a play, *The Guinea Outfit*, about life on board. I ask students to compare and contrast these disparate forms of evidence and at the end of this portion of the session I send them directly to the footnotes, at first to scan their variety and then to take a closer look at a few. Are they all in English? Are African voices represented, however obliquely? Why and why not? Is the transatlantic slave trade "global" as Rediker posits it? Do we get a sense of "the world" of slavery by studying the captain? What else would we need to know in order to amplify this picture? I bring the physical book to class (the students have just that one chapter on online reserve) and recommend it as postsemester reading, noting its subtitle (*A Human History*) and that it's published by a trade press, which likely means the author is interested in a wider reading public, like students, beyond their courses or their university education per se. I've also had students read an excerpt for that day from Saidiya Hartman's memoir, *Lose Your Mother*, her account of her trip to Ghana in search of the origins of the trade. I focus on this quote: "If the past is another country, then I am its citizen. I am the relic of an experience most preferred not to remember, as if the sheer will to forget could settle or decide the matter of history. I am a reminder that 12 million crossed the Atlantic Ocean and that the past is not over yet. I am a progeny of the captives. I am the vestige of the dead. And history is how the secular world attends to the dead."[4] I encourage students, via a back-and-forth discussion in which we unpack Hartman's text, to think about what kind of histories of slavery we've just encountered, how they reconcile and how they don't. I also show Hartman's memoir as part of my quest to get students to think of themselves as life-long history readers. My lecture material sets up the Indian Ocean–world slave system as well, and I draw contrasts and comparisons across these geographical spaces as part of my larger pedagogical purpose, which is to get students to focus on a big question via some particulars, both big and small, via historians and memoirists, via things that bring the multidimensionality of the global to bear. Though I have not yet had a chance to teach it, I have been told that Yvette Christianse's novel *Unconfessed* is a powerful teaching tool for units that seek to move beyond the empire of transatlantic slavery.[5]

In terms of where it occurs in my syllabus, this exercise is the first one of its kind I do, and it usually hooks students both to Rediker's text and to the exercise of close reading from top to bottom. I use some chapters of Isabel V. Hull's book *Absolute Destruction* later on in the course to achieve some of the same ends (see chapter 7 of this book, where I talk about how this work fits into my overall syllabus architecture).[6] In this instance I precirculate a list of questions and ask students to write out their answers on a separate piece of paper and bring them to class because we will be having a discussion on those questions in lecture. The two chapters we read, "Waterburg" and "Pursuit and Annihilation," are very dense and challenging, and I tell students so from the outset. I also tell them that they should use the questions (Who were the Herero, and what were the "atrocities" to which they were subjected? Why does Hull want to focus on "the slide from pursuit to outright annihilation" [p. 45]?) as guides to reading and that they might want to consider reading the passages highlighted twice, once for basic comprehension, once to answer the questions directly. And, of course, I am sure to tell students, do this work, it will be on the exam! This gets their attention, but so, frankly, does Hull's narrative. Some of my questions are very directional: for example, "Look at the quote from Trotha, pp. 42–43 [para. beginning 'The official history of the campaign . . .']. What does it tell us about Trotha and about German military imperial culture?" Other questions direct students to the footnotes themselves: "What evidence does she use to determine what happened? What role does African testimony play?" These questions lead to a discussion of the oral reports Hull uses, a discussion on their reliability and their entanglement in the very contexts of imperial culture and colonial war her story aims to tell. We talk about Hull's sensitivity to this, the power and the drama of the archive, the need to move beyond official records, and the perils of the whole enterprise. Because the seats in the lecture hall are nailed down, I am typically running up and own the aisles to get answers to my questions or to draw out a reluctant speaker; some don't bite, and that's fine too.

This archives exercise with Hull's book makes for one of the most exciting class sessions in the whole semester, for me and I think for students, too. The exercise has turned up on qualitative course evaluations as part of a memorable class session, and it can bring some students — especially those interested in cultures of war — into office hours as well. It's clearly an exercise you could pull off with an extract or two from any number of secondary works, to make any number of points about archival riches, interpretive license, the historian's role and responsibility, the humbling task of trying to write histories from below, histories without written archives, histories based in oral testimony, the power and perils of witness — all on a global scale or in the shadow of the global as historical framework. I recognize, too, that many world history teachers may not have ready access to monographic work or may lack the resources for reproducing large sections of it either in hard copy or in online venues. There are ways around these obstacles. The first is fairly low tech and low effort in terms of preparation. Choose a short passage from any text, display it overhead on a projector or computer screen, or, if possible, find an online version students can all access. Or make just a few copies that can be shared among pairs or groups. Even if students cannot access the footnote material, you may be able to, and you can make use of it in the lesson to help students ask questions about the conditions that produce the story or piece of evidence you have before you. Fragments of songs, snatches of poetry, excerpts from any form of media you have can be used in the service of archive talk. As I detail in chapter 8 ("Teaching 'Digital Natives'"), the internet is a fabulous source for just such fragments. Do you want to dramatize the mobility of indentured labor? Search for and find data sets from colonial archives, fragments of "coolie" song, excerpts from Amitav Ghosh's novel *Sea of Poppies*. Even if you can't get deep into a site, just bringing the student to its threshold can make for a great lesson in the archival quest, as the website featuring "The Dark Soul of the People: Slaves from Mauritius" and even Ancestry.com demonstrate.[7] With the major exception of material in Google books, you can print most of what you can find and use the URL to circulate materials. But, as I also caution above, surfer beware. You can't necessarily rely on these digital archives from one semester to the next. To quote *New York Times* contributor Patricia Cohen, "As research libraries and archives are discovering, 'born-digital' materials — those initially created in electronic form — are much more complicated and costly to preserve than anticipated."[8] The possibility of "digital extinction" looms large over all such projects, which disadvantages long-term curricular planning but serves as a very provocative reminder of the short life of so much historical evidence and its contingency on the vagaries of history itself, global or otherwise.

I'm a great believer in the use of novels as archival sources in world history, in part because I take a flexible view of what counts as evidence, and because I am interested in how structures of feeling and their histories end up being lodged in places where historians may not necessarily look. I think we should reach for readings that can dramatize historical processes and changes in ways that textbooks and even conventional sources can't always, or exclusively, do. So I've used Khushwant Singh's *Train to Pakistan*, Chinua Achebe's *Things Fall Apart*, and Rokeya Sakhawat Hossain's *Sultana's Dream* to leverage questions about partition, colonialism, and women's emancipation, either to dig down to the nitty-gritty of such questions or to ask how they have been represented. My choice of fiction and my use of it in lecture and discussion are not random. I use novels to sustain and forward arguments about events and themes I have purposefully sedimented throughout the course, rather than simply as "illustrations" of a particular place, culture, or time. This is a distinction worth lingering on, for dropping a novel into a world history syllabus does not, in and of itself, make your argument for the limits and possibilities of the global as an analytical category — let alone for the urgency of history as a critical method for assessing the global. Historians of Africa who wince when they hear that Achebe features on a world history syllabus are right to do so, if this is the only place Africa appears or if the novel stands in for conversations about the complexities of European colonialism and African community in all their specificity and variation in a global context. This is true, of course, of any piece of evidence you use to make a case for your vision of world history. Some evidence will be prismatic, shedding light on multiple spaces and maybe even manifesting interconnectivity across space, if not time. Other kinds of evidence will be more successful as orientation devices for more particular worlds, or as one piece in a composite picture you are trying to draw about an extended historical moment across various geographies. This is how I use *Train to Pakistan*. It is a partition novel, and a devastating one at that.[9] But I frame it as one example of the global phenomenon of partition, displacement, and segregation in and around the postwar, postcolonial period, ranging it alongside lectures and discussions about apartheid, the Iron Curtain, and the color line in the Jim Crow South. Above all, I suggest that the novel is one archive of the representation and experience of that period; that it should be placed alongside other forms of documentation and other evidence of the violence and historical impact and meanings of the time. I endeavor to make a case, in other words, for the novel as a way into thinking about global questions from a historical point of view, reminding students that though this is not a literature course, historians can read novels as a form of archive, especially if they subject those novels to the same forms of interpretive scrutiny they would any other source.[10]

I'm not sure my work with *Train to Pakistan* is totally successful, and I am continually revising and rethinking that lecture and the use of the novel in it. I've taken to admitting to this insecurity at the end of the lecture, which happens to come near the end of the course, a positioning which gives me the opportunity to think aloud from the podium about whether such arguments hold, how they compare to earlier platforms I've built (using the work of Marco Polo, Ibn Battuta, Las Casas, and other "coherent" texts), and the limits of using novels as historical sources. The response to my use of novels is mixed. On the one hand, undergraduate students don't have a well developed sense of genre, so they may not be fussed about juxtaposing fiction with other kinds of evidence. On the other hand, many students are quite conservative about what counts as history, which they see as more "scientific" than literature, especially if they are considering history as a major on the pathway to law as a career. In some iterations of my world history syllabus, I have asked students to produce archives of their own—oral histories of their grandparents' Second World War memories, for example, or of their parents' immigration stories. When those stories are part of the mix, I draw explicit comparisons across various evidentiary forms. The hardest task of all is to bring these questions back to the problem of the global and thinking historically about it. Our reliance on English as our medium is a huge handicap, though drawing attention to that fact can help fortify arguments across the syllabus about what globality really is. When we use novels, I always ask students to pick up the book and look at it in its totality. Who published it and when? What front and back matter is there to help us place it? How did it end up in our hands, through whose intervention and via what forms of global circulation? What, in other words, is the archive of which this is a piece, and what footnotes do we need to fully appreciate the novel as a global artifact, if it is one?

Some of these questions are mooted, others transformed, by the archives available on the web and by the various digital and print forms they may or may not end up taking (see chapter 8, "Teaching 'Digital Natives'"). When, for example, is a blog a historical source? Though I have not yet taught with it, I am intrigued by the possibilities of using the book *Baghdad Burning: Girl Blog from Iraq* in my world history course.[11] The pseudonymous author, known as "Riverbend," blogged "what she saw" in the war zone of Iraq beginning in 2003, and her posts have been edited, organized, and printed between covers. The possibilities for this text — as part of a unit on empire, as the basis for a discussion of war and embodiment, as an example of the historically contingent character of archives — seem endless. And, as in so many other places in my syllabus, the potential for learning as much from my students about these questions as from the material at hand is one of the things that makes the challenges of teaching world history virtually irresistible.

———— Chapter Ten ————

Testing (for) the Global

———————

I am ashamed to see what a shallow village-tale our so-called History is.
RALPH WALDO EMERSON

———————

IT TOOK ME LONGER than it should have to figure this out: how you test is critical to how, and even whether, students come away with the knowledge and the skills that the design of your syllabus has been aiming for. In retrospect, the belatedness of this realization is hard to believe because the connection is so commonsensical. And yet, the link between the content and shape of my course on the one hand and how I planned to concretize them via various forms of writing, thinking, and speaking (including exams) was not something I spent a lot of time on until comparatively recently. I think that has to do partly with the effort that goes into preparing—reading, searching for sources, retooling in areas where you have no expertise, thinking about and rearranging sections and subsections of the course—all of which can be time consuming, especially if you don't hew directly to a textbook line. Also, if you lecture from a podium as I do, there's a tendency to think in one mode, "me to them," a vector that mostly focuses on the pain of delivery and not enough on how to evaluate if the material is getting through. Testing can be almost an afterthought; or, rather, testing as a teaching tool, as opposed to simply an evaluation tool, may not be foremost in your mind, let alone at the front end of your syllabus planning.

I suspect that my comparative obliviousness to the pedagogical effects of testing can also be chalked up to my unexamined privilege as a Big Ten history professor. Those who teach to a test, especially the World History AP Exam, have a lot of their destinations mapped out for them, even if they exercise discretion with respect to the routes they use to arrive at those end-places. "Outcomes assessment," as a bureaucratic tool and a surveillance technology, has also come relatively recently to higher education, and the degree of its intrusiveness depends on where you teach and what your institution's commitments to and resources for monitoring outcomes are, whether in terms of evaluating general education or majors and minors. But until I began teaching world history in the context of accelerating contemporary rhetorics about the urgency of global curricula and institutional pressures for classes that enhance the student's "global competencies," I was not focused on specifying what the global could or should mean or how indispensable a tool historical thinking is for apprehending it. Testing has emerged for me as a critical component in my own syllabi only as a result of my designing the course explicitly around the meaning of the global and my desire to cultivate critical global-history thinking among students. And in ways I never anticipated when I began teaching world history two decades ago, the pressure of globalization in its late twentieth-century historical forms pushed me into a more robust and well-planned engagement with testing as part of the pedagogical, as opposed to the grading, process.

To think this question through I return, as I did in the introductory chapter of this primer, to first principles. Historical protocols are the driver, the means to an end: the most imaginative, if not also the best way to grasp what is claimed as, described as, and bundled up as the global of world history. This is not to say that I have a static or narrow view of what history is or does. To the contrary: the interdisciplinary power of history and its flexible methods make it appealing and adaptive, of course. Nor am I unaware of how entangled the profession and its procedures are with histories of global empire, capital, "civilization," and violence, nor of how vexing a task it is to constitute world history as a subject from North America, in this extended historical moment. But neither can we lie down in front of these questions or cede the ground to easy, additive models that don't problematize or, worse, take the idea of the global at face value rather than insist on its many and variegated historical forms, as well as on its limits as a category of analysis. I've tried to resist being excessively personal in this primer, but, for me, the purpose of world history is to enable students to learn how to read critically, to write analytically, and, above all, to appreciate more fully what it means to think like a historian — and, in this context, to think critically about the global. And while I have fallen short of sharing my entire History 100 syllabus, I want to be very specific here about how I have tried, within the constraints of my own classroom conditions, to make the testing part of the course a reflection of my global history principles and commitments. Through a series of assignments, whose aim is to impart to students a variety of reading, writing, and thinking skills, I grapple with three challenges that face all students of history: identifying the historical problem I want to tackle (the when and where of the global), deciding what methodologies are best suited to that problem (the "where do we see if from" question), and locating and making use of the primary sources necessary for analyzing the subject at hand (archives, evidence, and standards of persuasion).

It's not that I have tossed out the baby with the bathwater, dispensing with earlier assignments I had developed or creating mindblowing new ones to deal with these questions. Nor have I resorted, yet, to the strategy of one K-12 world history teacher, which is to hand out the final exam on day one of class and build toward it from there.[1] What I have done is to think harder about what kinds of assignments would help consolidate the ideas and themes from lecture and discussion in ways that "test" for both knowledge of fact and detail and push students to remember as they study and do the assignments that what they are doing is particular to the demands of a world history course. So, as with any lecture I give or syllabus section I design, I ask myself, Why does this belong in a world history course, as opposed to one I might teach about European empires or even Western civilization? And I don't shy away from talking to students directly about the links between what I am asking them to learn and the skills I want them to develop through the assignments they are doing. I also devote a lot of class time, up to one session per exam, to reviewing the exam preparation materials and talking through my expectations and pedagogical purposes.

Some of my understanding about the test as a teaching tool originated in response to the fact that at the University of Illinois, History 100 is required for Social Science Education majors, the future schoolteachers of Illinois. Depending on when the course is offered, there could be quite a critical mass of students enrolled, so this use of class time to address questions of testing and pedagogy seemed justified. Most recently I have begun to offer to meet with students individually or in groups, to give them the opportunity to raise questions they might have about my course design, pedagogical strategies, etc. — and of course to get their feedback and hear their ideas. But it didn't take long for me to realize that many students who had signed up for the course simply to fulfill a general education requirement or with a vague idea of being a history minor, also appreciated being clued in to the rationale behind the examinations I would be giving. In fact, those conversations themselves gave me some of the vocabulary — such as "pivot," "genealogy," and "interconnectivity" — that began as implicit or muted design principles and that I now see more clearly as part of my syllabus architecture. Thinking about testing and talking about testing for the global using historical methods help students hone their global thinking skills and may also help you clarify your own rationales for testing.

My testing has two basic components: the identification, or ID, and the extended response. These take place in handwritten, in-class settings, and they are the only portion of the evaluation process I supervise when I teach with TAs, who develop their own correlative syllabi with their own assignments, both quotidian and otherwise (students are normally required to do a three- to five-page paper in addition to short assignments, journaling, or both). Typically, and with lots of input from the TAs, I design three exams that are evenly spaced during the semester, and they cover material from each of the three major sections into which the syllabus is divided. The exams are cumulative, by which I mean they build on one another: the first one has only IDs, the second has IDs and short answers, and the third has IDs and essays. As I've indicated, I provide elaborate study sheets drawn directly from lecture outlines, readings, and discussions. If students have been coming to class, they see that their attendance and attention is rewarded, because there are few surprises. If they have not, they may be motivated between the first and second exam to be more attentive, though I have little reliable data on this point.

A word here on the handwritten exam in the age of very sophisticated digital possibilities and fast-moving social media forms: recent research links graphic facility to a whole set of developmental skills, including sequential thinking and memory, skills critical to thinking historically, and skills for a variety of other competencies.[2] Playing off the idea that there are skill-building links between hand and brain, my exams in world history operate from the premise that we need to cultivate students' gross *and* fine motor skills when it comes to thinking historically about the global. Beginning with IDs is a way to start with the gross motor skills. I give students a long list of possible IDs, up to seventy-five, and tell them they will have thirty of those seventy-five on the test, from which they must choose ten. On the review sheet, I say: "You will be asked to give date (2 points), place (2 points) and historical significance (6 points). 'Historical significance' has three dimensions: basic definition, deep factual explanation, and global interconnectedness. We will detail these in our review session. The purpose here is to learn the material and build some skills — namely, how to link the 'factual' information of an item with its global historical significance." This final sentence is written in bold font.

In the review session, I begin by modeling one or two IDs: here are the constituent parts; here's how you build the architecture of your response. No bullet points, no lists are allowed. Full sentences and a coherent paragraph are required for each identification. I tell students that especially since they have a list that contains all the IDs that will appear on the exam, we are looking for their capacity to show their knowledge of the facts, to manifest some deep or detailed knowledge of those facts, and, most important of all, to use those facts to make a case for interconnectedness. I say expressly, if I read an ID answer about the Mexican revolution that's totally internal to that event, the student will receive only partial points. That means the student should go back to the lecture notes and outline, and the textbook and readings for the day, and see how we made 1910 spin on multiple axes. I try to drive the same point home on the exam that I have been trying to make in lecture and through the larger course design: What makes this item global? Is it global? When is it? And how will you show me you know what that means? Because that's what we are looking for; that's how the student earns all six points for registering his or her understanding of "historical significance" in the context of world history.

My IDs range from commonly known personas to less familiar ones (Genghis Khan, Krotoa); from concepts to events (commodity racism, Versailles Treaty); and from places with specific histories to those with nodal possibilities (Elmina, Champagne fairs). Each one on the list is connected to several others, and I work hard in the review sessions to help students draw the links—sometimes literally, by diagramming on the chalkboard or an overhead projector.[3] For the first exam especially, I spend all the time students want, all the time they ask for, rehearsing the basic elements of each ID and narrating examples of what a complete answer would resemble, what its constituent parts are. I speak of gross motor skills—gathering date and place and memorizing those—and of finer skills as well, that ability to make something of the facts you have and construct a case for the global. I talk about this skill as history at work, and also about its portability as part of a skill set in all walks of life and in many professional settings. It's about digesting large bodies of material, but in a discriminating way, with a guide to the breadcrumbs and an emergent grid or sieve, interconnectedness, through which to sift the data. It's all true, and it's what thinking historically means in a 100-level course. Students seem surprised that I am apparently willing to give the whole game away.

Of course this is a sizeable expenditure of class time, of instructional unit time, that most precious of commodities these days, at least in public universities like my own. Yet what does it profit me to cover the whole globe and leave students with no apparatus for making sense of it, to move on without modeling skills, skills students probably already have some basis in, and pushing them to extend those skills to world history as an object of inquiry? Some excel at the first exam, some don't, as you might expect. We follow through with those who don't excel if they seek us out, and we keep explaining the system as we move into the next segment of the syllabus. Yes, I say in the lecture right after the first class, this term or event or process will be on the next exam, as an ID. I ask my students, "When I ask how you would analyze the term's global historical significance, what will you say? Let's talk about it now so when the exam comes all you have to do is review." By this time, if the student has been in the Hot Seat, I probably know her name and may have even met her in office hours as well.

The second exam builds, skill-wise, on the first. We still have IDs with the same protocols, but fewer of them to choose from and fewer required on the exam. We've added a short essay with instructions: "Be sure to (1) make an argument (10 points), (2) produce examples to support it, (10 points each), and (3) make a conclusion that addresses the historical significance and global interconnectedness of the question (10 points)." These directions are also on the study sheet, which lists a set of short-answer questions from which students will be asked to choose. Again, I spend considerable class time going over the study sheet, giving students a few possible constituent parts for building the IDs and short essays. In this exam prep, I tell students, "Be smart; look for IDs to prepare that will help you out in the short answer." Students can import one ID answer, not word for word but with overlapping details, into their short answer. I tell them, "Be sure your 'facts' are linked tightly and persuasively to your large point; think of the arcs of your argument." Or I warn students, "It's your turn! Remember how hard you were on Isabel Hull or Marcus Rediker for the unelaborated links between their evidence and their claims? It's hard, but it can be done, because (ahem) you've done the reading and come to lectures and have been in the Hot Seat and turned in all the worksheets. You have the goods, you need to perfect your writing/communication skills." And again, the emphasis is on combining fine and gross skills: facts and synthesis that explain, or at least describe, a global process, connection, or landscape.

Repetitio est mater studiorum. By the final exam many, if not most, of the students get it, and more than a few are in my office or in TA office hours with the study sheet before we talk about it in class. Students want to see if they are on the right track and whether their ideas for connection make sense. The last test contains fewer IDs and longer essays — three to four pages each, longhand, required. I give students both essay questions ahead of time and students have to do both. The same instructions that were given for the short answer apply to the essay questions, but between exam 1 and exam 2 students have done their three- to five-page paper, so they've already moved into a longer discursive format. In the last review session, I hammer away at the usual themes: fact, deep background, connection — links between facts and interpretation and between facts and a global view. My biggest fear about teaching History 100 is that at the end of the day, all the work that has gone into my design principles will slip away as students race past the exams for their grade, that students will come away with Emerson's "shallow village-tale" for their troubles and mine. My scheme is no guarantee against that, but it makes practical and intellectual sense to me as an extension of my vision about world history and its potential for equipping students with a distinctively historical approach to the global. As I often remind students, this isn't Introduction to Global Literature or A Survey of Global Sociology. We borrow from each of those domains, but history matters in its own way, and now the students know, hopefully, a little more about what that means.

Like most of the design principles in this primer, what I have sketched out is not rocket science. You can likely do it smarter than this, and probably do, especially if you prepare students for the World History AP exam. College and university professors have a lot to learn from a more outcome-based assessment model, though they may have more freedom to design as they will, and to match their syllabus ambitions with their diagnostic tests. I know only too well that students would like to hear that this project of testing for the global gets them all As, but that is not necessarily the case. I think testing does engage even those who don't get As in a processual experience in which the syllabus design and the way students get tested are integrated, if not perfectly so. As must be clear, the size of the course lecture I work in shapes, and indeed constrains, everything I do in my syllabus, from assignments to temporal frames to proactive learning components. And while I do get a few converts to the history major or minor at the end of the semester, I don't actually get stellar course evaluations. Not at all. I usually put them away for six months and return to them before I sit down to face my next world history syllabus design. I don't intend this to be flippant. We need better feedback mechanisms than a final course evaluation and better methods for figuring out how and why, or if, students learn globally when we teach world history. I have circulated pre-midterm evaluations to solicit responses to various aspects of the course, and I try to amend my methods accordingly, as well as take stock of the fit between my goals and their response. These are, of course, challenges for all teachers of history, a subject that has always had a tenuous hold in the secondary curriculum in the United States, and that, like all humanistic disciplines and subjects, is under pressure at the tertiary level precisely because of queries about what "real world" skills it delivers.[4]

Frankly, my goal is not to master the art of the "rate my professor" process, which tends to cater to student satisfaction as a consumer rather than to student learning per se.[5] At the same time, I certainly understand what the standardized teaching evaluation means for teachers' lives. In the face of this quantification of outcomes for the market place of higher education, I remain committed to trying to impress on students the benefits of stretching their minds beyond the first horizon and considering history — and more specifically, the benefits of historical thinking in a global mode — as one tool in their toolkit for a lifelong appreciation of what it means to live in this world. Those payoffs are, admittedly, hard to measure at the end of the semester because they take time to germinate, which means we have to range qualitative course evaluations against qualitative outcomes that are less verifiable statistically, but for which we need forms of assessment that match our intellectual and pedagogical goals, individually and collectively. Only then will our conversations truly be about the processes of learning, as well as the process of teaching world history.[6]

—— Epilogue ——

Never Done

IF EVER A VOLUME of poetry captured the terrors of undertaking a world history course, Adrienne Rich's *An Atlas of the Difficult World* does it. She has a line that sums up where you may feel we are at the end of this primer: "I promised to show you a map, you say, but this is a mural."[1] I would say, too, that the difference between a map and a mural is a small but instructive distinction. In this context, the map is to the textbook as the mural is to teaching: one is a source of information with directives, the other is live, an act of perpetual articulation, representation, and translation. The syllabus mediates the two. What I've tried to do in this primer is to show how syllabus design can free you from anxiety about the enormity of world history and return you — time and again — to dynamic interaction with its possibilities, and with a host of possible sources, our own historical times and places among them. The map is yours to use, the syllabus is yours to make. When the design is playful, as opposed to rigid or prescriptive, it allows for easy movement between genres, across scales, and through bodies of time and expanses of space. As Rich says simply and eloquently, "there are roads to take." There are always roads to take.

All those possibilities mean your syllabus is never done. I, for one, always keep what I call a "shadow syllabus" up and running on my computer desktop while I am teaching the introduction to world history. Compared to the well-oiled machine of a syllabus my students get at the beginning the semester, mine is a mess and legible only to me. It's filled with notes to self about what to read to learn more about X or to be able to answer someone's question about Y. It has random citations and URLs and snippets of text and images from here and there, many of which seemed urgently relevant at the time I found them but when returned to offer only glimmers of connection to the syllabus or its constituent parts. But I do return to that syllabus, especially at the end of the semester, because I know how kinetic and fluid all narrative accounts of the past are, not to mention how partial and occluded my view of the global is. I'm both resigned and resistant to that, which is why my shadow syllabus file is always open, never done — a digital equivalent, perhaps, of Rich's roads to take.

Despite my doubts about the capacity of my own world history syllabus to succeed as such, I remain committed to it as a pedagogical project because I think it has some capacity to cultivate skills that are valuable intrinsically and in the contemporary moment. For the sake of symmetry, if not artistry, here are 10 of those skills, in no particular order:

- an appreciation for the complexity of object and method, and for the global as both of these;
- a capacity to think, visualize, read, and communicate in several dimensions;
- an ambition to develop several kinds of competencies in order to stretch one's capacities beyond the first, most obvious horizon;
- a principled conviction about the capacities of historical thinking, broadly understood and applied;
- a respect for the boundaries of disciplinary knowledge; a correlative skepticism about their hallowed truths;

- a recognition of how congruent and competing methods produce new forms of knowledge and new objects of study;
- a recognition of how dynamic, in time and space, contemporary problems and their solutions necessarily are;
- a commitment to integrative interpretive frameworks, and a recognition of when the unassimilable, the fragment, also tells a story;
- a utopian sense of how engagement with difference (difference of method, interpretation, conviction, and experience) can unsettle and transform one's own practice
- an openness to the payoffs of deep knowledge, accrued over time and through cooperative struggle, argument, and even disagreement.

As secondary school teachers know better than anyone, building on these "habits of mind" takes time, and requires full-scale attention to the relationship between syllabus design and student learning—between theory and practice—that we give far too little time and even fewer resources to.[2] Teachers of world history have as much of an opportunity to realize all these skills, or to hone them, as their students do. As long as we critically engage with it, that reciprocity—between teacher and student, student and syllabus, knowledge and history, history and the world—is one reason to keep at it, even if we never get it completely right.

---- *Notes* ----

Introduction. Why Design?

1 Ted Kooser, "On the Road," in *Delights and Shadows* (Port Townsend, Wash.: Copper Canyon Press, 2004), 77.
2 A. Bartlett Giamatti, *The University and the Public Interest* (New York: Atheneum, 1981), 135.
3 See Tsing, *Friction*, 1.
4 Thanks to Dana Rabin for reminding me of this.
5 Thanks to Stephanie Foote for asking me this very question.
6 I draw here on Stephanie Foote's luminous essay, "Amateur Hour: Beginning in the Lecture Hall," *Pedagogy* 10, no. 3 (2010): 458.
7 See Hal Foster, *Design and Crime* (London: Verso, 2002), 20.
8 Meier, *The Power of Ideas*, 168.

One. Timing: When to Start

1 Now in the National Museum of Anthropology, Mexico City.
2 This is an echo of the title of a book by the anthropologist Johannes Fabian, *Time and the Other: How Anthropology Makes Its Object* (New York: Columbia University Press, 1983).
3 Abu-Lughod, *Before European Hegemony*; Gunder Frank, *Re-Orient*.
4 See Hobson, *The Eastern Origins of Western Civilization*.
5 Thanks to Marilyn Lake for this suggestion. For a great example, see the silversmith turned merchant in Brook, *The Troubled Empire*, especially 215.
6 Faroqhi, *The Ottoman Empire and the World Around It*, 14–16. For broader discussions of views of world history from outside the United States, see Manning, *Global Practice in World History*.

7   Pomeranz and Topik, *The World That Trade Created*, xiv.

8   Ibid., xiii.

9   Daniel A. Segal, "'Western Civ' and the Staging of History in American Higher Education," *American Historical Review* 105, no. 3 (2000): 770–805.

10 Kenneth Pomeranz, "Introduction: World History and Environmental History," in Burke and Pomeranz, *The Environment and World History*, 5.

11 For an important early take on this, see Bentley, "Sea and Ocean Basins as Frameworks of Historical Analysis."

12 Christian, *Maps of Time*.

13 Burke, Christian, and Dunn, *World History*, 3.

14 Kiernan, *Blood and Soil*. I am grateful to Nathan Chio for this reference.

15 One model for this, to which teenagers may relate, is V. Corzo-Duchardt, "Chains of Custody," in Mers, *Useful Pictures*, 46–57.

16 Segal, "'Western Civ' and the Staging of History in American Higher Education," 799.

Two. Centering Connectivity

1   Manning, *Navigating World History*, 82.

2   See Lynne Cheney, "Politics in the Classroom," *The History Place*, http://www.historyplace.com/pointsofview/cheney.htm.

3   Heidegger, quoted in Rey Chow, *The Age of the World Target: Self-Referentiality in War, Theory, and Comparative Work* (Durham: Duke University Press, 2006), 29.

4   I borrow here from Donald MacKennzie, *An Engine, Not a Camera: How Financial Models Shape Markets* (Cambridge: MIT Press, 2006).

5   Adrienne Rich, *An Atlas of the Difficult World* (New York: W. W. Norton, 1991), 6.

6   White, *The Middle Ground: Indians, Empires, and Republics in the Great Lakes Region, 1650–1815* (Cambridge: Cambridge University Press, 1991) and the Spatial History Project at Stanford University, http://www.stanford.edu/group/spatialhistory/.

7   See Cooper, "What Is the Concept of Globalization Good For? An African Historian's Perspective."

8   Karen Ho, "Situating Global Capitalisms: A View from Wall Street Investment Banks," in *The Anthropology of Globalization: A Reader*, edited by Jonathan Xavier Inda and Renato Rosaldo (Malden, Mass.: Blackwell, 2008), 137–64.

9   Akerman and Karrow, *Maps*, 65–68. See also Lewis and Wigen, *The Myth of Continents*.

10 Subrahmanyam, *Explorations in Connected Histories*, 4.

11 Tsing, *Friction*, 6.

12 Wright, *The World and a Very Small Place in Africa*.

13 Stearns, *Gender in World History*, 2.

14 Prestholdt, *Domesticating the World*. For a compressed version, see Jeremy Prestholdt, "On the Global Repercussions of East African Consumerism," *American Historical Review* 109, no. 3 (2004): 755–81.

15 Shoshana Keller, "Women's Liberation and Islam in Soviet Uzbekistan, 1926–1941," in Ballantyne and Burton, *Bodies in Contact*, 321–41.

16 See the Modern Girl around the World Research Group, *The Modern Girl around the World*.

17 Waltner and Maynes, "Family History as World History."

18 See Hamalainen, *The Comanche Empire*.

19 The quote is from the American political scientist Karl Deutsch (1912–1992), cited in Briggs and Burke, *A Social History of the Media*, 21.

20 I am grateful to a reader for Duke University Press for insisting on this point and helping me appreciate its stakes.

Three. How to Do More than "Include Women"

1 For one concrete example, see Strasser and Tinsman, "Engendering World History."

2 For primary sources that deal with both of these examples, see Hughes and Hughes, eds., *Women in World History v. 2*.

3 See Powers, *Women in the Crucible of Conquest*.

4 Jennifer Morgan, *Laboring Women*. Ned Blackhawk engages in a similar kind of speculative reconstruction in *Violence over the Land: Indians and Empires in the Early American West* (Cambridge: Harvard University Press, 2006), 17–18.

5 Sarah S. Hughes, "Gender at the Base of World History," in Roupp, *Teaching World History*, 85–88.

6 Roosevelt, *The Rough Riders*.

7 Adele Perry, "Reproducing Colonialism in British Columbia, 1849–1871," in Ballantyne and Burton, *Bodies in Contact*, 143–63.

8 Levin, *The Heart and Stomach of a King*.

9 Thanks to Clare Crowston for pressing this point.

10 In fact, the Comintern denounced them; see Smith, *Gender and the Mexican Revolution*, 24.

11 Allman and Tashjian, *"I Will Not Eat Stone."*

12 Grossman, "A Question of Silence: The Rape of German Women by Occupation Soldiers"; and Hyun Sook Kim, "History and Memory: The 'Comfort Women' Controversy," in Ballantyne and Burton, *Bodies in Contact*, 363–82.

13 Fitzgerald, *Big White Lie*, 198–99.
14 Students may respond better to the history of sexual norms than to that of gender norms. Strasser and Tinsman, "Engendering World History," 163.
15 Powers, *Women in the Crucible of Conquest*, 15.
16 This is Powers's interpretation in *Crucible of Conquest*.
17 Mitchell, *Colonising Egypt*, 95.
18 Roper, "Martin Luther's Body: The 'Stout Doctor' and His Biographers," 361.
19 See Ballantyne and Burton, *Bodies in Contact*, Ballantyne and Burton, *Moving Subjects*, and Kathleen Canning, "The Body as Method? Reflections on the Place of the Body in Gender History," *Gender and History* 11.3 (1999): 499–513.
20 For this class session, I use Lucy Eldersveld Murphy, "Native American and Metis Women as 'Public Mothers' in the Nineteenth Century Midwest," and Julia C. Wells, "Eva's Men: Gender and Power at the Cape of Good Hope," both in Ballantyne and Burton, *Bodies in Contact*, 164–82 and 84–105.
21 On "connective comparison," see the Modern Girl around the World Research Group, *The Modern Girl around the World*.

Four. World History from Below

1 Spier, *The Structure of Big History*.
2 Premo, *Children of the Father King*, 9.
3 All of my analysis here is borrowed from Cheek, *Mao Zedong and China's Revolutions*, 41–75.
4 See Midgely, *Women against Slavery*.
5 *The History of Mary Prince*.
6 Here "Asia" emphatically means China and India together, because of the shared commercial fate of tea and opium. For an express connection between these products and "coolie" labor, see Sharma, "'Lazy' Natives, Coolie Labour and the Assam Tea Industry."
7 Karl, *Staging the World*, chapter 5.
8 Quoted in Dominic Sachsenmaier, "Alternative Visions of World Order in the Aftermath of World War I: Global Perspectives on Chinese Approaches," in Conrad and Sachsenmaier, *Competing Visions of World Order*, 151.
9 Allman and Burton, "Destination Globalization?," *Journal of Colonialism and Colonial History* 4, no. 1 (2003). Thanks to Lynn Hunt for a timely reminder of this point.
10 I associate this skepticism about the impact of local stories, presumably small stories, with critics of women's and gender history as world history: What, I have been asked, can those histories possibly tell us in comprehensive terms about the

atom bomb? But I believe this skepticism is related to the question of the work of "the particular" in world history more generally.

11 Felix Driver and Raphael Samuel, "Rethinking the Idea of Place," *History Workshop Journal* 39 (1995): vi. Thanks to Tony Ballantyne for this reference.

12 Bu Bunh, *Red Earth*.

13 Lake and Reynolds, *Drawing the Global Colour Line*.

14 Jung, *Coolies and Cane*.

15 Azuma, *Between Two Empires*.

16 Linebaugh and Rediker, *The Many-Headed Hydra*.

17 Shepherd, *Maharani's Misery*.

18 See Marcus Rediker, "The Poetics of History from Below," *Perspectives*, September 2010, http://www.historians.org/perspectives/, and Marcus Rediker, *Between the Devil and the Deep Blue Sea: Merchant Seamen, Pirates, and the Anglo-American Maritime World, 1700–1750* (Cambridge: Cambridge University Press, 1993).

19 Berger, *South Africa in World History*, and Cohen, *East Asia at the Center*. See also Julia Clancy-Smith, "The Middle East in World History," in Dunn, *The New World History*, 293–300.

Five. The Event as a Teaching Tool

1 I draw on Restall, *Seven Myths of the Spanish Conquest*, and Bennett, *Africans in Colonial Mexico*, in this context.

2 Menocal, *Ornament of the World*.

3 Rebecca Overmyer-Velázquez, "Christian Morality in New Spain: The Nahua Woman in the Franciscan Imaginary," in Ballantyne and Burton, *Bodies in Contact*, 67–83.

4 Manela, *The Wilsonian Moment*.

5 Ibid. Irish nationalists were also present; see Pat Walsh, *The Rise and Fall of Imperial Ireland: Redmondism in the Context of Britain's Conquest of South Africa and Its Great War on Germany, 1899–1916* (Dublin: Athol, 2003), 485–88.

6 See Lake and Reynolds, *Drawing the Global Colour Line*.

7 See "Concept Map," Wikipedia, for a demonstration, or Mers, *Useful Pictures*, for a more elaborate discussion of its possibilities. I am grateful to Marie Ciavarella for these suggestions.

8 Weber, "Between Nationalism and Feminism: The Eastern Women's Congresses of 1930 and 1932."

9 Mitter, *Bitter Revolution*, 162.

10 Thanks to Marilyn Lake for helping me appreciate this point.

11 Stephen White, "Communism and the East: The Baku Congress, 1920," *Slavic Review* 33, no. 3 (1974): 492–514.

12 Stephens, *Black Empire*, 27–28.

13 Jason Knirk, "The Dominion of Ireland: The Anglo-Irish Treaty in an Imperial Context," *Eire-Ireland* 42, nos. 1 and 2 (2007): 241.

14 Brent Hayes Edwards, "The Shadow of Shadows." For a longer version of this chain of events, see Tony Ballantyne and Antoinette Burton, *Empires and the Reach of the Global, 1875–1955*, chapter 3, "Global Empires, Transnational Connections: Anti-colonialism and the Cross Currents of Modern Imperialism" (Harvard University Press, forthcoming).

15 "The Berlin-to-Baghdad Railway Convention (1903)," in Snyder, *The Imperialism Reader*, 348–56; see also Sean McMeekin, *The Berlin-Baghdad Express: The Ottoman Empire and Germany's Bid for World Power* (Cambridge: Harvard University Press, 2010).

16 Azuma, *Between Two Empires*, and Wells, *We Have Done with Pleading*.

17 Sanjay Subrahmanyam, "Introduction: Mughals and Franks in an Age of Contained Conflict," in Subrahmanyam, *Explorations in Connected Histories*, especially 1.

18 Abu-Lughod, "Going beyond Global Babble," 131.

Six. Genealogy as a Teaching Tool

1 Steven Ettinger, *Torah 24/7* (New York: Devora Publishing, 2003), 2.

2 A useful reference here is Schoonover, *Uncle Sam's War of 1898 and the Origins of Globalization*.

3 Hull, *Absolute Destruction*.

4 W. E. B. DuBois, "The African Roots of War," *Atlantic Monthly* 115, no. 5 (May 1915): 707–14. The full text can also be found at http://www.webdubois.org/.

5 Carlos Marichal, "The Spanish-American Silver Peso: Export Commodity and Global Money of the Ancien Regime, 1550–1800," in Topik, Marichal, and Frank, *From Silver to Cocaine*, 27.

6 See Sven Beckert, "Cotton: A Global History," in Bentley, Bridenthal, and Yang, *Interactions*, 48–63.

7 Brook, *Vermeer's Hat*, especially 152.

8 Ibid., 156.

9 Cited in Illona Linthwaite, ed., *Ain't I a Woman! Poems by Black and White Women* (London: Virago, 1987), 66.

10 Lyrics and music by Bernice Johnson Reagon, Songtalk Publishing Co., 1985; performed by Sweet Honey in the Rock, *Sweet Honey in the Rock, Live at Carne-*

gie Hall, recorded in 1987, issued by Rounder/Umgd in 1992, compact disc. The commodity story narrated in the song is not connected to any actual manufacturer or corporation. Thanks to Bernice Johnson Reagon for this information.

11 Roy, *Poverty Capital*.

Seven. Empire as a Teaching Tool

The epigraph is taken from Karl Liebknecht, "Where Will Peace Come From?" *Le Socialisme*, November 2, 1912.

1 Burbank and Cooper, *Empires in World History*, 3–4.

2 Sweet, *Recreating Africa*.

3 Johnson, *Where Good Ideas Come From*, 21–22.

4 Getz and Streets-Salter, *Modern Imperialism and Colonialism*, 1–9 and 129.

5 For much of what I have come to know and like about this approach, I am indebted to Anna Bateman and her lecture on the continental spaces of Russian imperialism called "Cheek by Jowl."

6 Nehru wrote, "Japan's re-awakening . . . sent a thrill through our Continent. Japan has shattered the white man's prestige in the Far East and has put all Western imperial powers on the defensive." See Lal, "The Concentration Camp and Development: The Pasts and Future of Development," 222.

7 Cemil Aydin, "A Global Anti-Western Moment? The Russo-Japanese War, Decolonization, and Asian Modernity," in Conrad and Sachsenmaier, *Competing Visions of World Order*, 213–36; Young, *Japan's Total Empire*, especially 88–95.

8 For some texts I have found useful in this regard, see Boahen, *African Perspectives on Colonialism*; Adas, *Prophets of Rebellion*; Nayar, *1857*; Dunn, *Resistance in the Desert*; Barkey, *Empire of Difference*; and Ballantyne and Burton, *Bodies in Contact*.

9 Balce, "The Filipina's Breast: Savagery, Docility, and the Erotics of the American Empire"; and Jennifer Morgan, "'Some Could Suckle over Their Shoulder': Male Travelers, Female Bodies, and the Gendering of Racial Ideology, 1500–1770," in Ballantyne and Burton, *Bodies in Contact*, 54–66.

10 Burbank and Cooper, *Empires in World History*, 55 and throughout.

11 Faroqhi, *The Ottoman Empire and the World Around It*, 25–26. Giancarlo Casale, *The Ottoman Age of Exploration* (New York: Oxford University Press, 2010).

12 Quoted in Hall, *Cultures of Empire*, 1.

13 Ishikawa, *Spain in the Age of Exploration, 1492–1819*, 23.

14 Williams, *Capitalism and Slavery*; Gretchen Gerzina, *Black London: Life Before Emancipation* (New Brunswick, N.J.: Rutgers University Press, 1995); Visram, *Ayahs, Lascars and Princes*.

15 For a compressed narrative version of this, see Antoinette Burton, "Women

and 'Domestic' Imperial Culture: The Case of Victorian Britain," in Boxer and Quataert, *Connecting Spheres*, 174–84.

16 On Tianjin and "concessionary imperialism," see Rogaski, *Hygienic Modernity*.

Eight. Teaching "Digital Natives"

1 Palfrey and Gasser, *Born Digital*, 1–7.

2 Lih, *The Wikipedia Revolution*, 3.

3 Ibid., 7.

4 Richard White, "What Is Spatial History?," available at http://www.stanford.edu/group/spatialhistory/.

5 Darnton, *The Case for Books*, xiv. On the decidedly unrevolutionary uses of digital media so far by professional historians in their capacity as researchers, see Robert Townshend, "How Is the New Media Reshaping the Work of Historians," *Perspectives in History* 48, no. 8 (November 2010): 35.

6 For one set of reflections on this, see Bodenhamer, Corrigan, and Harris, *The Spatial Humanities*.

7 Michalko, *Thinkertoys*, xix.

8 Mers, *Useful Pictures*, 32–45.

9 The site is available at http://worldhistoryconnected.press.illinois.edu/.

10 "The British in Bengal and Jamestown," lesson plan, available at http://state.virginia.edu/socialstudies/projects/jvc/unit/broad/bengal.html/.

11 Erik Vincent, "Learning to Think on Paper: Why Writing Remains Essential in an AP World History Course," *World History Connected* 7, no. 2 (June 2010), available at http://worldhistoryconnected.press.illinois.edu/.

12 Lynn Hunt, "The Art of History: How Writing Leads to Thinking (and Not the Other Way Around)," *Perspectives on History* (February 2010), available at http://www.historians.org/perspectives/. It also requires nuts and bolts attention; see Bill Strickland, "Improving Student Writing with Annotated Rubrics," in Roupp, *Teaching World History in the Twenty-First Century*, 79–82.

13 Jaron Lanier, "Does the Digital Classroom Enfeeble the Mind?" *New York Times*, September 16, 2010.

14 "Classes No Longer 'Paper-ful' Due to Internet Classwork," *Daily Illini*, April 12, 2010.

15 Kelly, *What Technology Wants*, 251.

16 Henry Jenkins, *Convergence Culture: Where Old and New Media Collide* (New York: New York University Press, 2006), 3. Thanks to Stephanie Foote for this reference. See also Robert B. Townshend, "How Is New Media Reshaping the Work of Historians?" *Perspectives on History* (November 2010): 31–36.

17 Thanks to Stephanie Foote for alerting me to the distinction between "intensive"

and "extensive" reading practices. See Briggs and Burke, *A Social History of the Media*, 53.

18 I draw here from Patrick Anderson, "Radical Intimacy: Dwight Conquergood's Classroom," *Cultural Studies* 21, no. 6 (2007): 815–20.

19 Kelly, *What Technology Wants*, 17.

Nine. Global Archive Stories

1 Anthony Grafton, *The Footnote: A Curious History* (Cambridge: Harvard University Press, 1997), 1–4.

2 See Antoinette Burton, ed., *Archive Stories: Facts, Fictions, and the Writing of History* (Durham: Duke University Press, 2005).

3 Rediker, *The Slave Ship*.

4 Hartman, *Lose Your Mother*.

5 For a good, short take on Indian Ocean–world slavery vis-à-vis the Atlantic system, see Gwyn Campbell, "Slave Trades and the Indian Ocean World," in Hawley, *India in Africa, Africa in India*, 17–51; and Christianse, *Unconfessed*.

6 Hull, *Absolute Destruction*.

7 Ancestry.com is especially useful as a teaching tool since it costs money to start; not all archives are "open." This means that students get a sense of the marketplace of digital media.

8 Patricia Cohen, "Fending off Digital Decay, Bit by Bit," *New York Times*, March 15, 2010.

9 Though I have not yet had a chance to use it in class, I recommend the Roli fiftieth anniversary edition (2007).

10 I've elaborated my view of these questions in *Dwelling in the Archive: Women Writing House, Home, and History in Late Colonial India* (New York: Oxford University Press, 2003).

11 Riverbend, *Baghdad Burning: Girl Blog from Iraq* (New York: Feminist Press, 2005).

Ten. Testing (for) the Global

Emerson is quoted in *Essays on the History of Blacks in Britain*, edited by Jagdish S. Gundara and Ian Duffield (Aldershot: Avebury, 1992), ix.

1 Laurie Schmitt, "The Nature of Civilization: A Final Exam," in Roupp, *Teaching World History*, 173–74.

2 Gwendolyn Bounds, "How Handwriting Trains the Brain: Forming Letters Is Key to Learning, Memory, Ideas," *Wall Street Journal*, October 5, 2010. The research on which the article is based is found in K. H. James and T. P. Atwood,

"The Role of Sensori-motor Learning in the Perception of Letter-like Forms: Tracking the Causes of Neural Specialization for Letters," *Cognitive Neuropsychology* 26, no. 1 (2008): 91–110. Thanks to Laura Mayhall for bringing this to my attention.

3 Thanks to Dana Rabin for reminding me of this point.

4 For a longer historical view of this in the context of teaching U.S. history, see Sam Wineburg, *Historical Thinking and Other Unnatural Acts.*

5 See Richard and Arum Josipa Roksa, *Academically Adrift: Limited Learning on College Campuses* (Chicago: University of Chicago Press, 2011).

6 Thanks to Laura Mayhall for encouraging me to think harder about these questions.

Epilogue. Never Done

1 Adrienne Rich, *An Atlas of the Difficult World* (New York: W. W. Norton, 1991), 6.

2 See Dale Griepenstroh, "A Week's Worth of World History Skills," in Roupp, *Teaching World History in the Twenty-First Century*, 153–61; and Meier, *The Power of Ideas*, 51.

—— Select Bibliography ——

Abu-Lughod, Janet. *Before European Hegemony: The World System, A.D. 1250–1350*. New York: Oxford University Press, 1989.
————. "Going beyond Global Babble." In *Culture, Globalization and the World System*, edited by Anthony D. King, 131–37. Minneapolis: University of Minnesota Press, 1997.
Adas, Michael. *Prophets of Rebellion: Millenarian Protest Movements against European Colonial Order*. Chapel Hill: University of North Carolina Press, 1979.
Akerman, James R., and Robert W. Karrow, eds. *Maps: Finding Our Place in the World*. Chicago: University of Chicago Press, 2007.
Allman, Jean, and Victoria Tashjian. *"I Will Not Eat Stone": A Women's History of Colonial Asante*. London: Heinemann, 2000.
Azuma, Eiichiro. *Between Two Empires: Race, History, and Transnationalism in Japanese America*. New York: Oxford University Press, 2005.
Balce, Nerissa. "The Filipina's Breast: Savagery, Docility, and the Erotics of the American Empire." *Social Text* 87 (2006): 89–110.
Ballantyne, Tony, and Antoinette Burton, eds. *Bodies in Contact: Rethinking Colonial Encounters in World History*. Durham: Duke University Press, 2005.
————. *Moving Subjects: Gender, Mobility, and Intimacy in and Age of Global Empire*. Urbana-Champaign: University of Illinois, 2008.
Barkey, Karen E. *Empire of Difference: The Ottomans in Comparative Perspective*. Cambridge: Cambridge University Press, 2008.
Bennett, Herman L. *Africans in Colonial Mexico: Absolutism, Christianity and Afro-Creole Consciousness, 1570–1640*. Bloomington: Indiana University Press, 2003.

Bentley, Jerry H. "Sea and Ocean Basins as Frameworks of Historical Analysis." *Geographical Review* 89, no 2 (1999): 215–24.

Bentley, Jerry H., Renate Bridenthal, and Anand A. Yang, eds. *Interactions: Transregional Perspectives on World History*. Honolulu: University of Hawaii Press, 2005.

Berger, Iris. *South Africa in World History*. New York: Oxford University Press, 2009.

Boahen, A. Adu. *African Perspectives on Colonialism*. Baltimore: Johns Hopkins University Press, 1987.

Bodenhamer, David J., John Corrigan, and Trevor M. Harris, eds. *The Spatial Humanities: GIS and the Future of Humanities Scholarship*. Bloomington: Indiana University Press, 2010.

Boxer, Marilyn J., and Jean H. Quataert, eds. *Connecting Spheres: Women in a Globalizing World, 1500 to the Present*. 2nd ed. New York: Oxford University Press, 2000.

Briggs, Asa, and Peter Burke. *A Social History of the Media: From Gutenberg to the Internet*. 3rd ed. London: Polity Press, 2009.

Brook, Timothy. *Vermeer's Hat: The Seventeenth Century and the Dawn of the Global World* London: Bloomsbury, 2008.

———. *The Troubled Empire: China in the Yuan and Ming Dynasties*. Cambridge: Harvard University Press, 2010.

Bu Bunh, Tran. *Red Earth: A Vietnamese Memoir of Life on a Colonial Rubber Plantation*. Athens: Ohio University Press, 1985.

Burbank, Jane, and Frederick Cooper. *Empires in World History: Power and the Politics of Difference*. Princeton: Princeton University Press, 2010.

Burke, Edmund III, and Kenneth Pomeranz, eds. *The Environment and World History*. Berkeley: University of California, 2009.

Burke, Edmund III, David Christian, and Ross E. Dunn. *World History: The Big Eras: A Compact History of Humankind for Teachers and Students*. Los Angeles: National Center for History in the Schools, UCLA, 2009.

Cheek, Timothy, ed. *Mao Zedong and China's Revolutions: A Brief History with Documents*. New York: Bedford, 2002.

Christian, David. *Maps of Time: An Introduction to Big History*. Berkeley: University of California Press, 2004.

Christianse, Yvette. *Unconfessed*. New York: Other Press, 2007.

Cohen, Warren I. *East Asia at the Center*. New York: Columbia University Press, 2001.

Conrad, Sebastian, and Dominic Sachsenmaier, eds. *Competing Visions of World Order: Global Moments and Movements, 1880s-1930s*. New York: Palgrave, 2007.

Cooper, Frederick. "What Is the Concept of Globalization Good For? An African Historian's Perspective." *African Affairs* 100 (2001): 189–213.

Darnton, Robert. *The Case for Books: Past, Present, and Future.* New York: PublicAffairs Books, 2009.

Dunn, Ross E. *Resistance in the Desert: Moroccan Responses to French Imperialism 1881–1912.* London: Croom Helm, 1977.

———, ed. *The New World History: A Teacher's Companion.* New York: Bedford, 2000.

Edwards, Brent Hayes. "The Shadow of Shadows." *Positions* 11 (2003): 11–49.

Faroqhi, Suraiya. *The Ottoman Empire and the World Around It.* London: I. B. Tauris, 2007.

Fitzgerald, John. *Big White Lie: Chinese Australians in White Australia.* Sydney: University of New South Wales Press, 2007.

Foote, Stephanie. "Amateur Hour: Beginning in the Lecture Hall." *Pedagogy* 10, no. 3 (2010): 457–70.

Getz, Trevor, and Heather Streets-Salter. *Modern Imperialism and Colonialism: A Global Perspective.* New York: Pearson, 2011.

Grossman, Atina. "A Question of Silence: The Rape of German Women by Occupation Soldiers." In *West Germany under Construction: Politics, Society and Culture in the Adenauer Era,* edited by Robert G. Moeller. Ann Arbor: University of Michigan Press, 1997.

Gunder Frank, Andre. *Re-Orient: Global Economy in the Asian Age.* Berkeley: University of California Press, 1998.

Hall, Catherine, ed. *Cultures of Empire: Colonizers in Britain and the Empire in the Nineteenth and Twentieth Centuries.* Manchester: University of Manchester Press, 2000.

Hamalainen, Pekka. *The Comanche Empire.* New Haven: Yale University Press, 2009.

Hartman, Saidiya V. *Lose Your Mother: A Journey along the Atlantic Slave Route.* New York: Farrar, Straus and Giroux, 2008.

Hawley, John C., ed. *India in Africa, Africa in India.* Bloomington: Indiana University Press, 2008.

The History of Mary Prince: A West Indian Slave Narrative. N.p.: CreateSpace, 2010.

Hobson, John M. *The Eastern Origins of Western Civilization.* Cambridge: Cambridge University Press, 2004.

Hughes, Sarah Shaver, and Bradley Hughes, eds. *Women in World History v. 2 — Readings from 1500 to the Present.* Armonk, N.Y.: M. E. Sharpe, 1997.

Hull, Isabel V. *Absolute Destruction: Military Culture and the Practices of War in Imperial Germany.* Ithaca: Cornell University Press, 2004.

Ishikawa, Chiyo, ed. *Spain in the Age of Exploration, 1492–1819*. Seattle: Seattle Art Museum, 2004.

Johnson, Steven. *Where Good Ideas Come From*. New York: Riverhead Books, 2010.

Jung, Moon-Ho. *Coolies and Cane: Race, Labor, and Sugar in the Age of Emancipation*. Baltimore: Johns Hopkins University Press, 2006.

Karl, Rebecca. *Staging the World: Chinese Nationalism at the Turn of the Twentieth Century*. Durham: Duke University Press, 2002.

Kelly, Kevin. *What Technology Wants*. New York: Viking, 2010.

Kiernan, Ben. *Blood and Soil: A World History of Genocide and Extermination from Sparta to Darfur*. New Haven: Yale University Press, 2009.

Lake, Marilyn, and Henry Reynolds. *Drawing the Global Colour Line: White Men's Countries and the Challenge of Racial Equality*. Cambridge: Cambridge University Press, 2008.

Lal, Vinay. "The Concentration Camp and Development: The Pasts and Future of Development." *Patterns of Prejudice* 39, no 2 (2005): 220–43.

Levin, Carol. *The Heart and Stomach of a King: Elizabeth I and the Politics of Sex and Power*. Philadelphia: University of Pennsylvania Press, 1994.

Lewis, Martin W., and Karen E. Wigen. *The Myth of Continents: A Critique of Metageography*. Berkeley: University of California Press, 1997.

Lih, Andrew. *The Wikipedia Revolution: How a Bunch of Nobodies Created the World's Greatest Revolution*. New York: Hyperion, 2009.

Linebaugh, Peter, and Marcus Rediker. *The Many-Headed Hydra: The Hidden History of the Revolutionary Atlantic*. London: Verso, 2000.

Manela, Erez. *The Wilsonian Moment: Self-Determination and the International Origins of Anticolonial Nationalism*. Cambridge: Harvard University Press, 2007.

Manning, Patrick. *Navigating World History: Historians Create a Global Past*. New York: Palgrave, 2003.

———, ed. *Global Practice in World History: Advances Worldwide*. Princeton: Markus Weiner, 2008.

Meier, Deborah. *The Power of Ideas: Lessons from a Small School in Harlem*. Boston: Beacon Press, 1995.

Menocal, María Rosa. *Ornament of the World: How Muslims, Jews, and Christians Created a Culture of Tolerance in Medieval Spain*. New York: Little, Brown, 2002.

Mers, Adelheid. *Useful Pictures*. Chicago: Whitewalls, 2008.

Michalko, Michael. *Thinkertoys: A Handbook of Creative-Thinking Techniques*. Berkeley: Ten Speed, 2006.

Midgely, Clare. *Women against Slavery: The British Campaigns, 1780–1870*. London: Routledge, 1992.

Mitchell, Timothy. *Colonising Egypt*. Berkeley: University of California Press, 1988.

Mitter, Rana. *Bitter Revolution: China's Struggle with the Modern World*. Oxford: Oxford University Press, 2004.

Modern Girl around the World Research Group (Alys Eve Weinbaum, Lynn M. Thomas, Priti Ramamurthy, Uta Poiger, Madeleine Yue Dong, and Tani E. Barlow). *The Modern Girl around the World: Consumption, Modernity, and Globalization*. Durham: Duke University Press, 2008.

Morgan, Jennifer. *Laboring Women: Reproduction and Gender in New World Slavery*. Philadelphia: University of Pennsylvania Press, 2004.

Nayar, Pramod K., ed. *1857: The Penguin Reader*. New Delhi: Penguin, 2007.

Palfrey, John, and Urs Gasser. *Born Digital: Understanding the First Generation of Digital Natives*. New York: Basic Books, 2008.

Pomeranz, Kenneth, and Steve Topik. *The World That Trade Created: Society, Culture and the World Economy, 1400 to the Present*. Armonk, N.Y.: M. E. Sharpe, 1999.

Powers, Karen Vieira. *Women in the Crucible of Conquest: The Gendered Genesis of Spanish American Society, 1500–1600*. Albuquerque: University of New Mexico Press, 2005.

Premo, Bianca. *Children of the Father King: Youth, Authority, and Legal Minority in Colonial Lima*. Chapel Hill: University of North Carolina Press, 2005.

Prestholdt, Jeremy. *Domesticating the World: African Consumerism and the Genealogies of Globalization*. Berkeley: University of California Press, 2008.

Rediker, Marcus. *The Slave Ship: A Human History*. New York: Vintage, 2007.

Restall, Matthew. *Seven Myths of the Spanish Conquest*. Oxford: Oxford University Press, 2003.

Rogaski, Ruth. *Hygienic Modernity: Meanings of Health and Disease in Treaty-Port China*. Berkeley: University of California Press, 2004.

Roosevelt, Theodore. *The Rough Riders*. 1889. New York: Scribner's, 1926.

Roper, Lyndal. "Martin Luther's Body: The 'Stout Doctor' and His Biographers." *American Historical Review* 115, no. 2 (2010): 351–84.

Roupp, Heidi, ed. *Teaching World History: A Resource Book*. Armonk, N.Y.: M. E. Sharpe, 1997.

———, ed. *Teaching World History in the Twenty-First Century: A Resource Book*. Armonk, N.Y.: M. E. Sharpe, 2010.

Roy, Ananya. *Poverty Capital: Microfinance and the Making of Development*. New York: Routledge, 2010.

Schoonover, Thomas. *Uncle Sam's War of 1898 and the Origins of Globalization*. Lexington: University of Kentucky Press, 2005.

Sharma, Jayeeta. "'Lazy' Natives, Coolie Labour and the Assam Tea Industry." *Modern Asian Studies* 43, no. 6 (2009): 1287–1324.

Shepherd, Verene, ed. *Maharani's Misery: Narratives of a Passage from India to the Caribbean.* Kingston: University Press of the West Indies, 2002.

Singh, Khushwant. *Train to Pakistan.* New Delhi: Roli, 2007.

Smith, Stephanie. *Gender and the Mexican Revolution: Yucatán Women and the Realities of Patriarchy.* Chapel Hill: University of North Carolina Press, 2009.

Snyder, Louis L., ed. *The Imperialism Reader: Documents and Readings on Modern Expansionism.* New York: D. Van Nostrand, 1962.

Spier, Fred. *The Structure of Big History: From the Big Bang until Today.* Amsterdam: Amsterdam University Press, 1996.

Stearns, Peter. *Gender in World History.* New York: Routledge, 2000.

Stephens, Michelle Ann. *Black Empire: The Masculine Global Imaginary of Caribbean Intellectuals in the United States, 1914–1962.* Durham: Duke University Press, 2005.

Strasser, Ulrike, and Heidi Tinsman. "Engendering World History." *Radical History Review* 91 (2005): 151–64.

Subrahmanyam, Sanjay. *Explorations in Connected Histories: From the Tagus to the Ganges.* Oxford: Oxford University Press, 2005.

———. *Explorations in Connected Histories: Mughals and Franks.* Oxford: Oxford University Press, 2005.

Sweet, James H. *Recreating Africa: Culture, Kinship, and Religion in the African-Portuguese World, 1441–1770.* Chapel Hill: University of North Carolina Press, 2003.

Topik, Steve, Carlos Marichal, and Zephyr Frank, eds. *From Silver to Cocaine: Latin American Commodity Chains and the Building of the World Economies, 1500–2000.* Durham: Duke University Press, 2006.

Tsing, Anna Lowenhaupt. *Friction: An Ethnography of Global Connection.* Princeton: Princeton University Press, 2005.

Visram, Rozina. *Ayahs, Lascars and Princes: The Story of Indians in Britain, 1700–1947.* London: Pluto Press, 1986.

Waltner, Ann B., and Mary Jo Maynes. "Family History as World History." In *Women's History in Global Perspective,* edited by Bonnie G. Smith, vol. 1, 48–91. Urbana-Champaign: University of Illinois Press, 2004.

Weber, Charlotte. "Between Nationalism and Feminism: The Eastern Women's Congresses of 1930 and 1932." *Journal of Middle East Women's Studies* 4, no. 1 (2008): 83–107.

Wells, Julia C. *We Have Done with Pleading: The Women's Anti-Pass Campaign.* Johannesburg: Ravan, 1991.

White, Richard. *The Middle Ground: Indians, Empires, and Republics in the Great Lakes Region, 1650–1815.* New York: Cambridge University Press, 1991.

Williams, Eric. *Capitalism and Slavery*. Chapel Hill: University of North Carolina Press, 1994.

Wineburg, Sam. *Historical Thinking and Other Unnatural Acts: Charting the Future of Teaching the Past*. Philadelphia: Temple University Press, 2001.

Wright, Donald. *The World and a Very Small Place in Africa: A History of Globalization in the Gambia*. Armonk, N.Y.: M. E. Sharpe, 1989.

Young, Louise. *Japan's Total Empire: Manchuria and the Culture of Wartime Imperialism*. Berkeley: University of California Press, 1998.

Index

iPad, 102
Iraq, 116

Japanese immigrants in California, 57
Joel, Billy, 73

Karl, Rebecca, 54
Kindle, 102
Kipling, Rudyard, 100
Kiva.org, 80

Lanier, Jaron, 102
Life and Debt (film), 80
Lih, Andrew, 96
Littorals, 19, 87
Local as teaching tool, 49; adding "thickness" and, 53; at the "bottom," 57–58; British tea drinkers example and, 52; Chinese nationalism and internationalism (nineteenth century) example and, 54; concerns with, 55–56, 59; decentering paradigms (us versus them) and, 58–59; Eurocentrism and, 53, 55, 58–59; ground-level examples and working up, 52; indentured migration example and, 56–57; indigenous communities and, 55; Japanese immigrant in California example and, 57; local versus global, 50–53; Mao example and, 51–52; pilgrimage examples and, 57; rebel leaders of eighteenth-century revolutions and, 50–51; rubber plantation workers example and, 56; sailors and ships and, 57–58; scale and perspective, 50–51; tea drinkers and, nineteenth-century British, 52–53; vertical connectivity and power and, 55–58; women in Bourbon Peru and, 51
Lose Your Mother (Hartman), 111
Louis XIV, 88–89

Maharani's Misery (Sheperd), 58
Manageability, 20
Manning, Patrick, 25
Mao, "Report on the Peasant Movement in Hunan" of, 51–52
Maps, 29–30
Maps of Time: An Introduction to Big History (Christian), 20
Maynes, Mary Jo, 33
Microfinance, 80
Middle Ground (White), 27–28
Mongol-Comanche example, 33–35, 87

Native Americans and colonizers, 27–28
Novels as archival sources, 113–15

The Ottoman Empire and The World Around It (Faroqhi), 18

Palfrey, John, 95–96
"Personal" global histories, 23, 115
Peru, 39, 51
Piedra del Sol (Stone of the Sun), 14–15
Pilgrimages, 57
Plagiarism and website citations, 99, 108
Prestholdt, Jeremy, 31
Prince, Mary, 53

Red Earth (Bunh), 56
"Report on the Peasant Movement in Hunan" (Mao), 51–52
Revolutions (eighteenth century), 21–22; rebel leaders and, 50–51
Rich, Adrienne, 127–28
Roosevelt, Theodore, gendered analysis of, 40–41
Rubber plantation workers (Indonesia), 56
Russian empire, 86
Russo-Japanese War, 87

ANTOINETTE BURTON is the Catherine C. and Bruce A. Bastian Professor of Global and Transnational Studies at the University of Illinois, Urbana-Champaign, where she teaches in the department of History. She is the author of *The Postcolonial Careers of Santha Rama Rau* (Duke, 2007); *Dwelling in the Archive: Women Writing House, Home, and History in Late Colonial India* (2003); *At the Heart of the Empire: Indians and the Colonial Encounter in Late-Victorian Britain* (1998); and *Burdens of History: British Feminists, Indian Women, and Imperial Culture, 1865–1915* (1994). Her edited books include *Empire in Question: Reading, Writing, and Teaching British Imperialism* (Duke, 2011); *Archive Stories: Facts, Fiction, and the Writing of History* (Duke, 2005); with Ania Loomba, Suvir Kaul, Matti Bunzl, and Jed Esty, *Postcolonial Studies and Beyond* (Duke, 2005); with Tony Ballantyne, *Bodies in Contact: Rethinking Colonial Encounters in World History* (Duke, 2005); *After the Imperial Turn: Thinking with and through the Nation* (Duke, 2003); *Majumdar, Janaki Agnes Penelope, 1886–1963* (2003); *Politics and Empire in Victorian Britain: A Reader* (2001); and *Gender, Sexuality, and Colonial Modernities* (1999). Her book *Brown Over Black: Race and the Politics of Postcolonial Citation* is forthcoming from Three Essays Collective, Delhi.

Library of Congress Cataloging-in-Publication Data

Burton, Antoinette M., 1961–
A primer for teaching world history : ten design principles / Antoinette Burton.
p. cm.
Includes bibliographical references and index.
ISBN 978-0-8223-5174-0 (cloth : alk. paper)
ISBN 978-0-8223-5188-7 (pbk. : alk. paper)
1. History — Study and teaching. 2. World history — Textbooks.
3. Civilization — History — Study and teaching. I. Title.
D16.2.B89 2012
907.1 — dc23   2011027452